A FLOWERING OF QUILTS

A FLOWERING OF QUILTS

Edited by
Patricia Cox Crews

University of Nebraska Press, Lincoln and London

This volume was published with
the support of a generous grant
from the Cooper Foundation.
The National Endowment for the
Humanities provided additional
support

Library of Congress Cataloging-
in-Publication Data
A flowering of quilts / edited by
Patricia Cox Crews.   p.   cm
Catalog of an exhibition of 53
quilts from the International
Quilt Study Center displayed
over a two-year period at the
University of Nebraska State
Museum. Includes bibliographi-
cal references and index.
ISBN 0-8032-1513-4 (cloth : alk.
paper) 1. Quilts–United States–
History–19th century–Themes,
motives–Exhibitions.
2. Botany in art–Exhibitions.
3. Ardis and Robert James
Collection–Exhibitions.
4. Quilts–Private collections–
Nebraska–Lincoln–Exhibitions.
5. International Quilt Study
Center–Exhibitions. I. Crews,
Patricia Cox. II. University of
Nebraska State Museum.
NK9112.F585   2001
746.46'074782'293–dc21
00-055957

N

This volume was published in
conjunction with the exhibition
"Fanciful Flowers: Botany and the
American Quilt," organized by
the International Quilt Study
Center at the University of
Nebraska–Lincoln.

University of Nebraska State
Museum, Lincoln
February 1999–March 2001

The Textile Museum,
Washington DC
23 February–3 June 2001

The Johnson Museum of Art,
Cornell University, Ithaca NY
30 June–6 August 2001

PRINTED IN CHINA

CONTENTS

ACKNOWLEDGMENTS

First, I would like to thank Ardis and Robert James. Their generosity led them to donate their extraordinary quilt collection to the University of Nebraska–Lincoln in 1997 to enhance public access to it and to provide students an opportunity to study quilts representing the history of quiltmaking in the United States from the early 1800s to the present. The Jameses' vision and munificence also led to the establishment of the International Quilt Study Center at the University of Nebraska–Lincoln. The center encourages the interdisciplinary study of all aspects of quiltmaking and fosters preservation of this worldwide tradition through the collection, conservation, and exhibition of quilts and related materials. Without the Jameses' public-mindedness and generosity, we would not have this unique resource at the University of Nebraska to share in the form of exhibitions and publications with the citizens of this state and nation and with people from around the world.

It is with sincere appreciation that I also acknowledge two liberal financial contributions to this project: The generous support of the Cooper Foundation made it possible to produce and sell this book with more than fifty color illustrations, and support from the National Endowment for the Humanities made it possible to complete the photography required for the color images of the quilts.

INTRODUCTION

Patricia Cox Crews

This publication presents the fifty-three quilts displayed over a two-year period at the University of Nebraska State Museum in an exhibition entitled "Fanciful Flowers: Botany and the American Quilt." Every six months thirteen botanically inspired antique quilts from the International Quilt Study Center's Ardis and Robert James Collection were showcased in the museum's Cooper Gallery for public viewing. In addition, one of the collection's most valuable quilts, the extremely fragile Baltimore Album quilt (plate 7), was displayed for a limited period during the first two months of the exhibition. The exhibition was curated by Carolyn Ducey, curator of the International Quilt Study Center, and by Susan Curtis, a curatorial assistant for the center during the year preceding the exhibition's opening.

This publication provides quiltmakers, collectors, textile scholars, and all readers interested in the study of American decorative arts an opportunity to view and examine in greater depth a selection of nineteenth-century quilts with floral motifs from the James Collection. The quilts selected for this exhibition, a number of which had never before been publicly displayed, comprise a range of styles, including cut-out chintz appliqué quilts (*broderie perse*–style quilts), album-style quilts (including a high-style Baltimore album quilt), a number of red-and-green floral appliqué quilts, as well as a limited number of pieced quilts and crazy quilts. The venue for this exhibition, a natural history museum, provided the impetus for examining the influence of gardening and botanizing (the collecting of plant specimens for study) on nineteenth-century quilt designs.

With that theme in mind, I invited Dr. Margaret Bolick, curator of botany for the University of Nebraska State Museum, and Susan Curtis, a curatorial assistant for the International Quilt Study Center, to contribute essays to this publication that pertain to two broad topics: women and the study of botany in the nineteenth century and the influence of gardening, which was traditionally women's work, on nineteenth-century quilt designs.

In her essay Margaret Bolick notes that botany became *the* science for American women during the nineteenth century and that the University of Nebraska was a "primary institution for training female botanists" (4). According to Bolick only Smith and Wellesley

Colleges produced more women botanists than the University of Nebraska, and the author offers some discerning explanations for this phenomenon. She also examines the interesting similarities and differences between female students of botany and quiltmakers from the period when gardening, studying plants, and creating elegant floral-patterned quilts became fashionable pastimes for many Victorian women.

Susan Curtis, an avid gardener and student of textile history, describes the striking parallels between flower garden design preferences of the nineteenth century and quilt designs and styles favored by American quiltmakers at that time. She observes that a formal design was preferred in gardens during the first quarter of the nineteenth century, and, likewise, quilts of the period usually exhibit a symmetrical format. By the end of the century, naturalistic gardens were favored, and crazy quilts, with their random placement of pieces and asymmetrical format, were the rage among quiltmakers.

The last section of the publication is a catalog of the quilts displayed for the "Fanciful Flowers" exhibition. Each color plate is accompanied by a detailed description of the quilt that was written by Carolyn Ducey, curator of the International Quilt Study Center at the University of Nebraska–Lincoln. Ducey highlights the appliqué, piecing, and quilting techniques as well as the historical, horticultural, and botanical influences evident in the design and execution of each quilt. Thoughtful research that addressed the technological, stylistic, botanical, and historical influences of the period coupled with a careful analysis of each quilt informs Ducey's descriptions, and, in turn, her descriptions help the reader note details about each quilt that might otherwise be overlooked.

When scanning the captions associated with each quilt pictured in this catalog, it immediately becomes clear that, as is typical of most collections, the majority of the quilts entered the center's James Collection without solid provenance. The Jameses assembled their collection primarily by purchase from dealers, and they maintained careful records that provide information about where a quilt was found. This dealer information is often the only clue to the possible place of origin of a particular quilt. However, the U.S. population has always been a mobile one; therefore, we cannot be sure that a quilt was made in the state where it was found by a dealer or collector. Consequently, Carolyn Ducey and I have very conservatively assigned place of origin for each quilt in this catalog. If we have only a dealer's note as to where a quilt was found and no other supporting clues or documentation, we designated place of origin as "possibly made" in the state where the dealer or the Jameses indicated the quilt was found. If we found information—such as stylistic clues within the quilt itself—to support place of origin as being the state where the dealer noted the quilt was found, we designated place of origin as "probably made" in that state. If the quilt entered the collection without a dealer's or collector's note on its provenance, then we simply designated it as "probably made in the United States" (or the eastern or southern United States if stylistic clues suggested a possible or probable tie to a particular region).

Ducey and I also searched for similar quilts published in the myriad books emanating from the statewide quilt surveys of the 1980s and 1990s as well as in the catalogs of the notable quilt collections of the Museum of American Folk Art, The Metropolitan Museum of Art, and the Maryland Historical Society, to name a few. The examination of quilts with solid provenance published in these books proved helpful in showing which quilt styles enjoyed national popularity (red-and-white floral appliqué) and which ones appeared to be regional styles (the cut-out chintz appliqué quilts of the southern plantations, for example). In this way other published catalogs proved to be useful resources for determining the quilts' probable place of origin. In some cases the books also made it clear that "probably made in the United States" was the only attribution we could confidently assert, because similar quilts were made by women (and occasionally men) in many states across this nation.

The catalog section includes basic information about every quilt and is arranged, in general, chronologically and by style. Whether a textile historian, a quilt historian, or merely a reader interested in American decorative arts, we invite you to page through the history and fanciful flowers of these nineteenth-century botanically inspired quilts.

WOMEN AND PLANTS
in Nineteenth-Century America

Margaret R. Bolick

The connection between women and plants is perhaps as old as human history.[1] This link took on a scholastic aspect in the late eighteenth and early nineteenth centuries, when botany became *the* science for women to study in the United States.[2] At about that same time, botanical images became increasingly common in American quilts.[3] There is not enough information on the lives of individual quilters to provide evidence that women who studied botany were more likely to use floral patterns in their quilts. However, scholarship in the last twenty years documents several types of feminine interactions with the plant kingdom that were considered to be a conventional part of women's domestic role during Victorian times. Gardening, studying plants, and creating elegant floral-patterned quilts became fashionable pastimes for Victorian women. By the end of the nineteenth century, women could study botany at universities and teach it at the secondary level.

PRE-NINETEENTH CENTURY LINKS BETWEEN WOMEN AND PLANTS

Knowledge of plants in prehistoric societies and early civilizations was inextricably linked to people's needs for food and medicine.[4] At least some elements of feeding and nursing the family were women's work in most cultures, so women needed a basic, practical knowledge of herbs and plant foods. Paleoanthropologists surmise that women were often the primary gatherers of plant foodstuffs; some even hypothesize that the first agricultural cultivation of plants was done by women.[5] Later, in societies where agriculture was defined as a male activity, women's role in food procurement shifted to gardening—herbs, vegetables, and ornamentals.

A feminine tradition of practicing herbal medicine goes at least as far back as medieval times and was one of the factors that linked botany and women.[6] Until very recently, most of the drugs used to fight disease came directly from plants or were derived from plant compounds. A pharmaceutical arsenal based on chemically synthesized drugs is a late nineteenth- to mid-twentieth-century development.[7] This early dependence on plants for medicinal purposes meant that botanical knowledge was essential for any medical practitioner until the twentieth century. The close ties between botany and medicine are illustrated by the fact that the two leading figures in American botany during most of the 1800s, John Torrey and

Asa Gray, were trained as physicians. But the widespread availability of adequately trained men of medicine was also a relatively late development, and one that depended on the patient's location and class. Even after physicians and apothecaries became relatively common in urban areas in the late eighteenth and early nineteenth centuries, in rural areas women were still the primary medical caregivers.[8]

BOTANY AS *THE* SCIENCE FOR WOMEN

The status of botany as the preferred science for feminine study developed in the early nineteenth century.[9] Prior to that, upper-class and aristocratic women, like their male counterparts, prescribed to the Enlightenment emphasis on all areas of science.[10] Their interests were either not directed to any particular scientific discipline or were directed to one such as chemistry. Maria Edgeworth, a domestic novelist known among literary and scientific circles, wrote in 1795: "Chemistry is a science particularly suited to women, suited to their talents and their situation."[11] Discussing Georgian Britain, the historian Patricia Phillips notes: "Botany, on the other hand, was a field not yet appropriated by the ladies, although the Queen, her mother-in-law, the Dowager Princess of Wales, and George III were keen botanists."[12]

Several factors in addition to a royal stamp of approval from Great Britain's Queen Charlotte contributed to the increasing association of botany and women in Great Britain and the United States.[13] Some of the reasons for studying botany were given in the writings of the time. When Jean Jacques Rousseau's 1771 *Essais éleméntaires sur la botanique* (Elementary essays on botany) was translated into English,

the title was changed to *Elements of Botany Addressed to a Lady*.[14] Rousseau approved of a mother teaching her daughter botany because it "abates the taste for frivolous amusements, prevents the tumult of the passions, and provides the mind with a nourishment which is salutary."[15] The late-eighteenth-century science writer Priscilla Wakefield added that "botany is a branch of Natural History that possesses many advantages; it contributes to health of body and cheerfulness of disposition, by presenting an inducement to take air and exercise."[16]

In the United States botany became *the* science for women perhaps more so than it did in other countries.[17] Emanuel D. Rudolph, a botanist and historian of botany, attributed this to the work of Almira Hart Lincoln Phelps.[18] Science was an important part of education in the home during the nineteenth century, and mothers often taught their children botany and other sciences.[19] Many of the books in common use were written by Almira Hart Lincoln Phelps, whose influence on nineteenth-century science education has been documented by scholars such as Emanuel D. Rudolph, Sally G. Kohlstedt, Lois B. Arnold, and Nancy G. Slack.[20] Almira was the youngest of a family of seventeen children that resided in Connecticut. She was close to her sister Emma Hart Willard and followed her into education. When her first husband died, leaving her with two small children to support, Almira Hart Lincoln accepted her sister's offer to come teach with her at a girls school in Troy, New York. While teaching at Mrs. Willard's school, both women became protégés of botanist Amos Eaton, who taught at the Rensselaer School, also in Troy. There was a lack of suitable science textbooks for schools at this time, and with Eaton's encouragement, Almira Hart Lincoln began her attempts to fill this need; she eventually wrote texts for every area of science except astronomy. Her first book was *Familiar Lectures on Botany*. Published in 1829, it went through nine editions and had sold more than 375,000 copies by 1872.[21]

Botany was also popular among women because there was the prevailing belief that the study of this science was congruent with contemporary views of acceptable, home-centered roles for women.[22] The scholar Marina Benjamin lists the desirable goals for late-eighteenth-century women as: "making domestic life comforting for family and friends, forming and improving the manners and conduct of the opposite sex, and teaching children."[23] In the early nineteenth century "the domestic idyll grew to embrace home and garden, and botany became the most moral of sciences."[24]

However, women's participation in botany as a science rather than as a domestic pursuit such as gardening was limited to amateur status by these same conventional roles. For example, the founding president of Vassar College believed that science education for women was valuable because it trained them to be better wives and mothers: "Physiology, chemistry, physics, and the various branches of natural history—have all of them a womanly side, and may be taught throughout, with reference to practical application, in women's acknowledged domain."[25] Lincoln Phelps's mentor, Eaton, was more blunt, being known to have said: "A woman is of no value, if she is not valuable at home; and she is worthless as a fungus, if she is not more interested in the concerns of her home, than in the concerns of all the rest of the world."[26]

Women, especially those with a familial relationship to a male botanist, could serve as facilitators of serious, "masculine" research: they could collect, enumerate, and illustrate specimens.[27] Ann Shteir's 1996 book *Cultivating Women, Cultivating Science: Flora's Daughter and Botany in England, 1760 to 1860* gives numerous examples of women as botanical helpmates in that country. In the United States Maria Martin Bachman assisted her naturalist husband in his collaboration with John James Audubon and painted the background plants and insects for two of the volumes of *The Birds of America*.[28] Kohlstedt gleaned the names of female plant collectors from the correspondence of Philadelphia botanist William Darlington.[29] Women independent of a male figure also became absorbed in the science. In Canada Catharine Parr Traill collected plants and supported her husband and children by her popular writings on Canadian botany and natural history.[30] In Australia Louisa Meredith illustrated her own books on the natural history of New South Wales and Tasmania.[31]

With a few exceptions these women did not do work that would lead to scientific papers and publications (as opposed to popular or educational writings) until late in the nineteenth century;[32] the professionalization of American botany in the last half of the nineteenth century excluded most women. Daniel Goldstein, a historian of science, analyzed the Smithsonian's network of correspondents and noted that as American science became more professionalized the level of communication between professional and amateur scientists declined; the contributions and position of the amateurs were reduced to marginal status.[33] However, by the beginning of the twentieth century women in a few hospitable institutions, particularly the women's colleges and western universities, began to earn the credentials that had become a prerequisite for a professional scientific career.[34]

Encouraging women to study botany always carried the risk that some of the students

would develop an interest in the subject that might go beyond the conventional into the professional. According to Ricky Clark, author of *Quilted Gardens: Floral Quilts of the Nineteenth Century,* the popularity of classic floral quilts peaked from the 1840s to the 1870s; women during that time also applied their womanly interests in plants and gardening to quilting. But for the next generation of girls an interest in plants would have coincided with both the increasing professionalization of the discipline of botany and greater opportunities in higher education for women.[35] Pursuit of botany in a paid position increasingly required at least a baccalaureate degree, however. The historian of science Margaret Rossiter has traced the baccalaureate origins of women scientists listed in the 1938 edition of *American Men of Science*.[36] According to her research, only the womens colleges Smith and Wellesley graduated more women botanists than the University of Nebraska.[37] Why was Nebraska

such a primary institution for training female botanists? Did these women who studied botany in an academic setting share characteristics with the women who a generation earlier had expressed their interest in plants through quilting?

Several factors may have contributed to the training of such a large number of women in botany and other sciences at Nebraska. Rossiter notes that the coeducational institutions that trained the largest number of female PhDs were midwestern and western schools rather than those of the eastern seaboard.[38] She proposed that rapidly growing fields in science might have been more receptive to women and that perhaps new and rapidly growing western institutions were also more receptive to women.[39] A third factor that could have affected the number of women in science was an influential professor who supported the admission and training of women.[40] The

Fig. 1. An 1895 photo captioned "after dinner in the lab" shows botany professor Charles Bessey, second from right, with a group of women science students. Entomologist Lawrence Bruner is pictured on the far right, and registrar Ellen Smith sits on the right in the front row. Courtesy of the University of Nebraska State Museum.

University of Nebraska had such a faculty member as its botanist from 1884 to 1915, Charles E. Bessey.

The University of Nebraska developed an exceptional program in botany during Bessey's tenure. It was one of the top four institutions to graduate botanists whom *American Men of Science* noted as being among the top researchers in their field at some point in their careers.[41] Bessey was proud of his efforts as an educator and published a list of his former students in a 1910 issue of the University of Nebraska's alumni magazine.[42] He kept a slightly different list in his files, one that included students who had not gone on to careers in botany. By combining these lists and checking the Bessey Papers in the University of Nebraska Archives for additional students, I compiled a list of 42 female students of this professor of botany between 1889 and 1911. Including other women who were listed in alumni records as receiving a Bachelor of Science degree or as botany graduate students in university catalogs during this time added another 110 women. (A Bachelor of Science degree awarded by the university during this time period did represent a science major, although it is not clear what level of concentration in a particular scientific discipline was required.) The alumni directories provided additional information about their husbands' names, their occupations, and their places of residence. The early university catalogs also gave each undergraduate's hometown and listed graduate students' area of study. The 1895 catalog specifically listed the students' place of birth, home county at the time of matriculation, and parents' occupation.

Bessey's effectiveness in welcoming women can be estimated by first comparing the percentage of women in his lists with the percentage of women who received a Bachelor of Science degree during the same time period and by then looking for a drop in the proportion of female science students after his death. Bessey's list of students was 28 percent women during a time when 23 percent of science degrees were given to females. Records in the 1926 alumni register show that the percentage of women science majors dropped to a little over 10 percent in the eleven years after his death (1916–26).

COMMON GROUND: QUILTERS AND FEMALE STUDENTS OF BOTANY

Ricky Clark profiles a typical quiltmaker as a woman of Protestant, European heritage, someone whose "parents or grandparents were probably born in the eastern United States or were European immigrants, most likely from Germany."[43] The early Nebraska quilters profiled by Patricia Crews and Michelle James had similar heritages. The five most common ethnic backgrounds of the early Nebraska quilters were German, English, Irish, Scottish, and Czech.[44] Almost all (97 percent) of the students enrolled at the University of Nebraska were born in the United States; Germany, with nine students, contributed the largest number of enrollees not born in this country. Of the non-immigrants, 36 percent were born in Nebraska, and another 60 percent were from midwestern or northeastern states. About half (49 percent) of the students resided in Lancaster County, where the university is located, when they first registered. The 1893 and 1895 catalogs explained that 40 percent of these students were from families that had moved to Lincoln temporarily for their children's education. The figures for the female science majors are similar; 51 percent listed Lincoln as their residence.[45]

Clark also shows in *Quilted Gardens* that most quiltmakers lived in a postfrontier rural area.[46] Like the quilters, many of the women science majors at the university had a rural background; 19 percent were from towns with a population of less than one thousand. Another 17 percent were from towns with fewer than four thousand residents. If one assumes that the 40 percent of the students whose families were temporary Lincoln residents were from rural areas, 56 percent of the women students came from towns smaller than ten thousand.[47] The science students were also a mobile group. Only 17 percent returned to their hometown after graduation, while more than one-quarter of them lived in a large urban center such as New York, Chicago, or Los Angeles.

In contrast, 87.5 percent of the Nebraska quilters of this time lived in the country or small towns.[48] But improvements in transportation helped influence the cultural uniformity of nineteenth-century quilters by making more widely available both fabrics and popular books and magazines. The publications were particularly important because they helped create and establish the norms for female behavior and spread the quilt patterns quickly.[49]

A final characteristic that many quilt-makers had in common was that their male relations were either farmers or artisans. For the women enrolled in university science courses, however, the proportion of families in which the parents were farmers was smaller. Of the parental occupations listed in the 1895 student catalog, 24 percent were farmers, 22 percent were professionals (doctors, lawyers, clergy, bankers), 26 percent were involved in commercial interests, 14 percent were skilled craftsmen, and the remaining 14 percent worked in a variety of skilled occupations (auditor, bookkeeper, railroad employee, surveyor). The ability to pay a child's tuition

and other university expenses suggests that most of the families were relatively affluent.

There are some striking differences between the students and the quilters as well. Only 11 percent of the Nebraska quilters surveyed by Crews and James went to college, and, by definition, all of the botany students did.[50] At a time when wife and mother were still seen as the primary roles for women, most Nebraska quilters married.[51] In contrast, 41 percent of the women who studied botany and the other sciences remained single. Twenty percent of these single women remained at home. Of those female students who did marry, 57 percent did not leave an alumnae record of work.[52]

Working outside of the home was uncommon for middle- and upper-class women of this time; the female science students were unconventional enough that 87 out of the 152 (58 percent) worked in the public sector—at least before they were married. They were conventional enough, however, that most of them (51 of those 87, or 58 percent) worked at the job considered most acceptable for

Fig. 2. Students from the University of Nebraska on a field trip in 1895. The rigors of fieldwork would not have surprised young women accustomed to rural life. Courtesy of the University of Nebraska State Museum.

women: teaching school. This was also the most common occupation among the quilters studied by Crews and James who worked outside the home.[53] Thirteen of the eighty-seven alumnae working in the public sector (15 percent) worked as technicians for government laboratories, an area Rossiter identified as "women's work" in science.[54] The stereotype of botany as an acceptable subject for feminine endeavor shows up here again: eleven of these thirteen female lab technicians were hired in plant specialties.

The remaining twenty-three women working in the public sector (26 percent) were highly unconventional, becoming college science professors, physicians, a chiropractor, a pharmacist, and an osteopath—all professions that were dominated by men until the 1970s. This unconventionality had its cost; less than one-third of these women married. Interestingly, five of the six who did marry were medical professionals who could practice outside of institutional bounds. Only one female professor married, and from the timing of her marriage it was probably after she had tenure. As with the technicians, the professorial positions show the effects of sex-role stereotypes. Of the eleven women who were college professors, seven were in botany and two were in other feminized sciences, home economics and hygiene.

*

In the mid–nineteenth century the same cultural influences that made flowers and leaves a favored design for quilts deemed botany an acceptable science for women to study. A generation beyond the era of classic floral quilts, women with similar backgrounds had the option of studying botany at some colleges and universities. The botany program at the University of Nebraska, a young school that had its setting in a largely rural state, provided an exceptional opportunity for some of these women to acquire the academic credentials that had become a prerequisite for employment as a botanist. Nonetheless, the women who pursued careers as professional scientists tended to do so at the cost of marriage and children. Their generation had no chance to have it all.

NOTES

1. Margaret Alic, *Hypatia's Heritage* (Boston: Beacon, 1986), 13.

2. Emanuel D. Rudolph, "How It Developed that Botany Was the Science Thought Most Suitable for Victorian Young Ladies," *Children's Literature* 2 (1973): 92–97.

3. Ricky Clark, *Quilted Gardens: Floral Quilts of the Nineteenth Century* (Nashville TN: Rutledge Hill, 1994), 4.

4. A. G. Morton, *History of Botanical Science* (London: Academic Press, 1981), 1.

5. Charles B. Heiser Jr., *Seed to Civilization* (Cambridge: Harvard University Press, 1990), 14; Morton, *History of Botanical Science*, 3.

6. Alic, *Hypatia's Heritage*, 56; Barbara Ehrenreich and Deirdre English, *Witches, Midwives, and Nurses: A History of Women Healers* (Old Westbury NY: Feminist Press, 1973), 14; Ann B. Shteir, *Cultivating Women, Cultivating Science: Flora's Daughters and Botany in England, 1760 to 1860* (Baltimore: Johns Hopkins University Press, 1996), 37–39.

7. Edward Kremers and George Urdang, *History of Pharmacy* (Philadelphia: J. B. Lippencott Company, 1940), 378; Walter H. Lewis and Memory P. F. Elvin-Lewis, *Medical Botany* (New York: John Wiley & Sons, 1977), vii–viii; Oswald Tippo and William L. Stern, *Humanistic Botany* (New York: W. W. Norton & Company, 1977), 211.

8. Kremers and Urdang, *History of Pharmacy*, 195.

9. Rudolph, "How It Developed," 92–95.

10. Alic, *Hypatia's Heritage*, 77–134; Patricia Phillips, *The Scientific Lady: A Social History of Women's Scientific Interests, 1520–1918* (London:

Weidenfeld and Nicolson, 1990), 27–47; Shteir, *Cultivating Women*, 137–85.

11. Quoted in Marina Benjamin, "Elbow Room: Women Writers on Science, 1790–1840," in *Science and Sensibility: Gender and Scientific Inquiry, 1780–1945*, ed. Marina Benjamin (Oxford: Basil Blackwell, 1991), 35.

12. Phillips, *The Scientific Lady*, 97.

13. Shteir, *Cultivating Women*, 36–37.

14. Rudolph, "How It Developed," 92.

15. Cited in Rudolph, "How It Developed," 92.

16. Cited in Rudolph, "How It Developed," 93.

17. Rudolph, "How It Developed," 94–95.

18. Rudolph, "How It Developed," 94.

19. Sally G. Kohlstedt, "Parlors, Primer, and Public Schooling: Education for Science in Nineteenth-Century America," *Isis* 81 (Sept. 1990): 425–45.

20. Rudolph, "How It Developed"; Sally G. Kohlstedt, "In from the Periphery: American Women in Science, 1830–1880," *Signs* 4 (autumn 1978): 81–96; Lois B. Arnold, *Four Lives in Science: Women's Education in the Nineteenth Century* (New York: Schocken Books, 1984); Shteir, *Cultivating Women*.

21. Arnold, *Four Lives*, 37–67.

22. Arnold, *Four Lives*, 59–60; Shteir, *Cultivating Women*, 63–64.

23. Benjamin, "Elbow Room," 40.

24. Benjamin, "Elbow Room," 42.

25. Quoted in Kohlstedt, "In from the Periphery," 88.

26. Quoted in Arnold, *Four Lives*, 59–60.

27. Kohlstedt, "In from the Periphery," 83–89; Arnold, *Four Lives*, 4–6; Shteir, *Cultivating Women*, 173–93.

28. Arnold, *Four Lives*, 25–35.

29. Kohlstedt, "In from the Periphery," 84–87.

30. Marianne G. Ainley, "Science in Canada's Backwoods: Catharine Parr Traill," in *Natural Eloquence: Women Reinscribe Science*, ed. Barbara T. Gates and Ann B. Shteir (Madison: University of Wisconsin Press, 1997), 79–97.

31. Judith Johnson, "The 'Very Poetry of Frogs': Louisa Anne Meredith in Australia," in *Natural Eloquence: Women Reinscribe Science*, ed. Barbara T. Gates and Ann B. Shteir (Madison: University of Wisconsin Press, 1997), 98–115.

32. Nancy G. Slack, "Nineteenth-Century American Women Botanists: Wives, Widows, and Work," in *Uneasy Careers and Intimate Lives: Women in Science, 1789–1979*, ed. Pnina Abir-Am and Dorinda Outram (New Brunswick NJ: Rutgers University Press, 1987), 78–103.

33. Daniel Goldstein, "Yours for Science: The Smithsonian Institution's Correspondents and the Shape of the Scientific Community in Nineteenth-Century America," *Isis* 85 (Dec. 1994): 573–99.

34. Margaret W. Rossiter, *Women Scientists in America: Struggles and Strategies to 1949* (Baltimore: Johns Hopkins University Press, 1982), 1–37.

35. Clark, *Quilted Gardens*, 3, 72–77.

36. Rossiter, *Women Scientists*, 11.

37. Rossiter, *Women Scientists*, 146–47.

38. Rossiter, *Women Scientists*, 34.

39. Rossiter, "Sexual Segregation," 146–55.

40. Rossiter, *Women Scientists*, 31–33.

41. Stephen S. Visher, *Scientists Starred, 1909–1943*, in "American Men of Science" (Baltimore: Johns Hopkins University Press, 1947), 173.

42. Charles E. Bessey, "Alumni Tidings: Botanists," *University Journal* (Nebraska) 7, no. 3 (1910): 42–43.

43. Clark, *Quilted Gardens*, 5.

44. Patricia C. Crews and Michelle M. James, "Continuity and Change in Nebraska Quiltmakers, 1870–1989," *Clothing and Textiles Research Journal* 14, no. 1 (1996): 7–15.

45. I compiled these statistics from the information I gathered from university catalogs and alumni magazines.

46. Clark, *Quilted Gardens*, 5.

47. Hometowns were listed in university catalogs. The town populations were taken from *Clason's Guide Map of Nebraska* (Denver: Clason Map Company, 1916).

48. Crews and James, "Continuity and Change," 10.

49. Clark, *Quilted Gardens*, 72–77.

50. Crews and James, "Continuity and Change," 9.

51. Patricia Cox Crews, personal communication.

52. Throughout this section, I have compiled the

statistics from data obtained from the University
of Nebraska alumni directories for 1912, 1918, 1928,
and 1926 and the *University Journal.* I consulted the
Nebraska Alumnus for noted changes in employment,
marital status, or address for each of the women.

    53. Crews and James, "Continuity and Change," 10.

    54. Rossiter, *Women Scientists,* 60–63.

BLESSED BE GOD FOR FLOWERS
Nineteenth-Century Quilt Design

Susan Curtis

Beautiful things are suggestive of a purer and higher life, and fill us with a mingled love and fear. They have a graciousness that wins us, and an excellence to which we involuntarily do reverence. If you are poor, yet pure and modestly aspiring, keep a vase of flowers on your table, and they will help to maintain your dignity, and secure for you consideration and delicacy of behavior.

Godey's Lady's Book and Magazine, March 1861

One of the most pervasive influences in the lives of nineteenth-century women was the dominance of gardening and floriculture. Women cultivated flower gardens to demonstrate their homemaking skills and to benefit from the genteel exercise gardening provided. They studied botany to fill their leisure time with productive activity and to understand the spirituality of nature. And by using floral motifs in their decorating, women believed that they could educate and provide moral guidance for their families.

Women incorporated nineteenth-century aesthetic sensibilities and motifs into all aspects of their creative work, whether they were designing flower gardens, quilts, home decorations, or clothing. An explosion of gardening and ladies' publications, driven by lower manufacturing costs and improved distribution methods, developed in the early part of the century. Popular trends were quickly disseminated through these magazines. Patterns for flower gardens, quilt blocks, embroidered flowers, knitted and crocheted flowers, floral hair weavings, lace floral designs, or wax flowers were published in every issue.

WOMEN'S ROLE IN NINETEENTH-CENTURY AMERICA

With the advent of the machine age and the shift in population from rural to urban areas, women found themselves with more leisure time and new social expectations. Instead of participating in the physical production of food and cloth, women became consumers of goods and services. In addition, the growing middle class believed the responsibility for the family's moral, spiritual, and educational growth lay within the woman's realm. Women were taught that one way they could safeguard their family's well-being was by surrounding them with beautiful things. And in nineteenth-century America, a motif felt to be inherently beautiful was anything floral.

The doctrine of natural theology, prevalent throughout the century, promoted the idea that to understand nature was to understand God. The New England transcendentalist movement, through its influential leaders Ralph Waldo Emerson and Henry David Thoreau, taught that nature held spiritual significance. It promoted gardening as a means of individual fulfillment and of being symbolically united with God. Therefore, to incorporate floral designs in her decorating would suggest that a woman and her family were morally and spiritually enlightened.

In addition to spiritual education, the cultivation and study of flowers was considered an excellent activity for women and children, providing gentle exercise and productive use of their leisure time. In fact, botany was the only natural science encouraged for participation by nineteenth-century women. By mid-century the overwhelming majority of amateur botanists were women, prompting the editors of *Science* magazine to write an article in 1887 titled "Is Botany a Suitable Study for Young Men?"[1] Men found themselves forced to refute the idea that males who studied botany were effeminate. The *Science* editors argued that botany was a sophisticated hobby that could divert young men from unsuitable leisure activities and vice. Nevertheless, women remained dominant in the field of botany until the beginning of the twentieth century, when the professional study of botany sharply split from amateur study.

GARDENING AND FLORICULTURE IN NINETEENTH-CENTURY AMERICA

Several developments led to the growing number of flower gardens in nineteenth-century America. First, with the increasing discovery of medical cures, women no longer had to focus their gardening efforts on the cultivation of medicinal plants. Second, the importation of South American and Mexican "tropical" plants, such as nasturtiums and zinnias, in mid-century created a taste for brilliantly colored, exotic flower beds. Because the plants could be grown from seed, they proved economical enough to be treated as annuals. Mail-order seed companies first appeared in 1806, and soon cockscomb, impatiens, and four-o'clocks filled flower beds with their vibrant colors.

In addition to annuals, gardeners planted bulbs and tuberous flowers in masses. Tulips and narcissus quickly became popular items of commerce in American garden nurseries. By the end of the nineteenth century, the Linnaean Garden in Long Island, New York, produced six hundred varieties of tulips.[2] Dahlias, another flower imported from Mexico, became the rage for nineteenth-century gardeners. By the middle of the century, garden catalogs devoted more space to varieties of dahlias than to any other species. Dahlias remained the most popular flower for massing in beds throughout the second half of the century. And as exotic flowers became popular in garden beds, they also began to appear in the quilts of the time. For example, see the Cockscomb quilt with a tulip border (plate 21) and the Baskets of Flowers quilt with dahlia-like flowers (plate 29).

Finally, writers for a variety of nineteenth-century publications extolled gardening as an important activity for all Americans, not

only for wealthy landowners. Walter Elder stressed in his 1848 publication, *The Cottage Garden of America*, that gardens were important because they were "refining and moralizing [to] the young" and "exalt the national character."[3] Andrew Jackson Downing, the son of a New York nurseryman and supporter of the transcendentalists, became an enormously popular garden designer and author of gardening books.[4] He wrote in his 1842 book, *Cottage Residences*, that beautiful homes and gardens would ultimately serve a moral purpose as "an unfailing barrier against vice, immorality and bad habits."[5] Downing also published a gardening journal, *The Horticulturist, and Journal of Rural Art and Rural Taste*, which offered advice on garden design, architecture, and flower lore.

American gardeners considered Italian, French, Dutch, and English gardens the epitome of style and strove to duplicate them throughout the eighteenth century. Differences in climate between Europe and North America, however, made the exact replication of gardens difficult, if not impossible. Beginning in the first quarter of the nineteenth century, American gardeners began to depart from the rigidly geometric style of Greek architecture popular in eighteenth-century gardens. They adopted a more natural design

with the encouragement of editors of popular gardening books and magazines.

In 1806 Bernard M'Mahon published the first American gardening book, *American Gardener's Calendar; Adapted to the Climate and Seasons of the United States*, in response to the frustration American gardeners experienced using European gardening advice and models.[6] In addition to advice on plant selection and garden design, M'Mahon offered a mail-order seed catalog at the back of his book. M'Mahon's publication was soon followed by numerous gardening books and periodicals.

Women could apply ideas from these publications to both motifs and layouts in their quiltmaking activities. The vining flower bed illustrated in the 15 September 1895 issue of *Gardening* magazine (see figure 3) parallels the quilt borders often seen during this century. Both the Whig Rose Variation quilt (plate 23) and the Mexican Rose quilt (plate 35) incorporate this same undulating border with leaves and blossoms. The floral shape of the flower bed design from the 15 April 1896 issue of *Gardening* magazine (see figure 4) could easily be used as a pattern for the floral appliqués seen in quilts like the Floral Wreath (plate 36) and the Floral Wreath with an animal border (plate 46). The influence of

Fig. 3. Garden design from Washington Park, Chicago. Taken from *Gardening*, 15 Sept. 1895, p. 5.

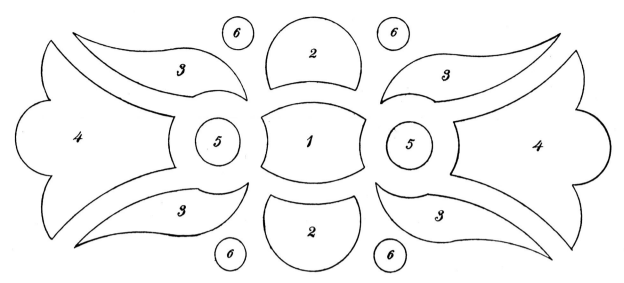

the garden design from an 1841 issue of *The Gardener's Magazine* (figure 5) may be noted in the design of the floral blocks in the Texas Star Variation with Tulips quilt (plate 37).

Individual flower species were important throughout the nineteenth century. In addition to their beauty, flowers were notable for the symbolism attached to each species and the lessons that could be taught through them. Flowers were often imbued with human characteristics and used in moral lessons. In 1847 N. Cleaveland translated and published *Flowers Personified, being a translation of "Les Fleurs Animées"* by Monsieur Grandville. In this book, flowers are transformed into human beings, and moral lessons are taught from their joys and sorrows. The story of Tulipia, exotically dressed in a Turkish costume constructed of flower petals and leaves, is one of a beautiful woman who becomes the sultan Shahabaam's favorite. But Tulipia neglects to improve herself and is tossed aside in favor of Rose-Pompon, who is intelligent and entertaining. Not only is Tulipia replaced as the chief sultana, she is put into a sack and dropped into the sea. For a few days the demise of the beautiful Tulipia is

the talk of the sultan's court. Then she is forgotten. The moral of the tale is that "beauty without intelligence leaves few traces on the memory."[7] *The Horticulturist, and Journal of Rural Art and Rural Taste* printed a three-page review and excerpts of the book, ending the review with the remark, "To such of our fair readers as do not already possess this ingenious and agreeable work, we beg leave to recommend it as one of the most attractive literary novelties of the season."[8]

In the June 1861 issue of *Godey's Lady's Book and Magazine*, Harland Coultas published the article "Flowers, and What May Be Learned from Them." In his article, Coultas illustrates the passage of human life through the life cycle of a flower and the wonder of all nature through its growth: "A flower is a beautiful world in itself. It is formed from the matter of the earth and atmosphere which is attracted about a seed, and every atom moves to its place in accordance with the operation of irresistible laws. There is no chance work in the building up of a flower. Now it only requires an enlargement of mind to see that the same principle applies to the world."[9]

Fig. 4. Flower bed design published in *Gardening*, 15 Apr. 1896, p. 231.

Fig. 5. Garden design from *The Gardener's Magazine*, July 1841, p. 351.

Early Christian artists and seventeenth- and eighteenth-century painters often used floral symbolism in their work. They used selected flowers to represent death and the transitory nature of human life. American folk artists also used this symbolic floral imagery in mid-nineteenth-century mourning paintings. They incorporated roses, pansies, and violets into portraits to symbolize death, remembrance, and humility (because in death we are made humble before God).[10] However, in the nineteenth century, floral symbolism grew beyond religious meaning into a broadly recognized cultural language.

Beginning in the 1830s, "dictionaries" deciphering the "language of flowers" were published. As the popularity of sending secret, romantic messages through flowers spread, dozens of books, usually written by women, quickly appeared. However, there was no standardization of the flowers' meanings, and many of these dictionaries contained contradictory definitions. For example, a yellow rose in one dictionary might denote infidelity in the recipient, while in another it asked forgiveness for the sender, and in

yet another it symbolized jealousy. Adding further to the confusion, a rose in Christian art had long symbolized martyrdom, whereas in American folk-art mourning paintings it symbolized death, and in the secular language of flowers the rose could mean anything from "war" to "meet me by moonlight." Society expected the sophisticated middle-class lady and gentleman of the nineteenth century to be well versed in the language of flowers, but all had to hope that their friends were using the same dictionaries.

THE TIES BETWEEN NINETEENTH-CENTURY FLOWERS, GARDENS, AND QUILTS

Nineteenth-century women had many opportunities to blend their interests in floral symbolism, floriculture, gardening, and quiltmaking. The beautiful and detailed color illustrations of flowers published in William Curtis's *Botanical Magazine* may have provided inspiration for design and color choices in their quilts. Perhaps Curtis's drawing of a pink, as seen in figure 6, inspired floral quilt motifs such as the nine large flowers in the Whig Rose Variation quilt (plate 14). The simple star shape of a coreopsis he sketched (figure 7) is discernible in the border flowers of the Flowers and Buds quilt (plate 27). Most floral- and garden-design illustrations in garden magazines of the period were simple line drawings that could have been easily copied and adapted for appliqué quilt pieces.

Design preferences for nineteenth-century flower gardens are similar to those seen in nineteenth-century quilts. American garden design in the first quarter of the nineteenth century emulated the formal design preferred in European gardens of the period. The *parterre de broderie*, first used in seventeenth-

Fig. 6. *Dianthus Chinensis*, China or Indian Pink. Sketch reproduced from *The Botanical Magazine, or, Flower-Garden Displayed*, 1793, volume 1, plate 25. Archives and Special Collections, University of Nebraska–Lincoln Libraries.

Fig. 7. *Coreopsis Verticillata*, Whorled Coreopsis. Sketch reproduced from *The Botanical Magazine, or, Flower-Garden Displayed*, 1796, volume 5, plate 156. Archives and Special Collections, University of Nebraska–Lincoln Libraries.

century Italian gardens, became a favorite garden design throughout America. In gardens using *parterre de broderie* style, serpentine beds were cut into an expanse of lawn and filled with shrubs or flowers. The style was meant to imitate embroidered fabrics and oriental rugs. At the same time, *broderie perse* quilts, like the cut-out chintz appliqué quilts in plates 3 and 4, were at the height of their popularity. As in the *parterre de broderie*–style gardens, makers of these so-called *broderie perse* quilts used small groups of chintz flowers appliquéd onto a whole cloth background. In both the *parterre de broderie*–style garden and the *broderie perse* quilt, the designer incorporated groups of flowers onto a plain background to reproduce the look of embroidered textiles. The name *broderie perse* references Persian embroidery and is believed to be a twentieth-century name

for this style of quilt.[11] It is interesting to note, however, that a related term was used in the nineteenth century to describe a garden style.

In 1827 *Gardener's Magazine* published highlights of a lecture delivered by R. R. Reinagle entitled "Original Beauty of Lines and Forms." The article described general design theory, which the magazine editors then applied to gardening. Parallels can also be observed in quilt designs of the period. Reinagle's essay builds on the axiom that every beautiful object is characterized as "something that is a well-ordered whole, in opposition to something that is in a state of chaos or confusion."[12] Both gardeners and quilters followed this axiom until the last quarter of the nineteenth century. To illustrate one point of his theory, Reinagle explains that straight lines

radiating from a center point or object form a pleasing shape. Even more visually pleasing are curving lines radiating from a center.[13] Both of these are common design formats seen in nineteenth-century floral quilts such as the Rose of Sharon quilt (plate 24) and Mexican Rose quilt (plate 34). Additionally, quilts throughout the first three quarters of the nineteenth century, such as the Floral Appliqué quilt (plate 30) and another Mexican Rose quilt (plate 35), were designed as symmetrical, well-ordered wholes, like their contemporary flower gardens.

In 1841 A. J. Downing published *A Treatise on the Theory and Practice of Landscape Gardening, Adapted to North America; with a View to the Improvement of Country Residences*. Through this book he promoted the new English garden design called *gardenesque*. According to excerpts published in an unsigned review of his book in an 1841 issue of *The Gardener's Magazine*, Downing defined *gardenesque* style as one in which each tree and flower bed must be able to stand alone in its artistic merit but, more important, must work together in the landscape to create a unified whole. He explained that the object is "to produce highly elegant and polished forms."[14] In addition, Downing espoused the theory that symmetrical designs are more pleasing. His description of *gardenesque* style parallels that of album quilts, in which the quiltmaker strives to provide an overall feeling of a harmonious whole from quilt blocks of dissimilar design. Album quilts, such as the Baltimore Album quilts (plates 7 and 8), rose to their height of popularity between approximately 1840 and 1860.

Fig. 8. A basket flower bed at Egandale (Highland Park IL). Taken from *Gardening*, 1 Oct. 1895, p. 19.

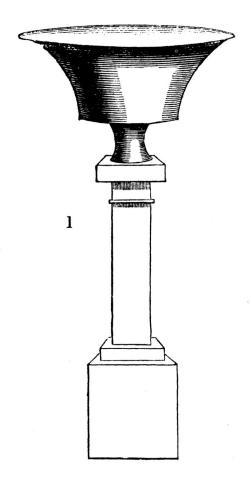

Fig. 9. Flower-basket illustration used throughout *The Gardener's Monthly* in 1862.

Figs. 10A and 10B. Illustrations of urns published in *The Gardener's Magazine*, Jan. 1835, pp. 12–13.

These quilts were not usually created for everyday use. More often they were presentation quilts. And paralleling the emphasis on detail in the *gardenesque* style of gardening, album quilts exemplify some of the most exquisite artisanship and needlework of the period.

Baskets of flowers were another common motif in nineteenth-century quilts. In gardening, Humphrey Repton, an English garden designer, developed a popular design for flower beds in the 1820s called basket flower beds. They were a bed of mixed flowers planted in a lawn and enclosed by a wicker, wood, or iron framework. (See figure 8.) These basket flower beds were incorporated into the gardens of both villas and cottages and were described several times by the Englishman J. C. Loudon in the 1830s and 1840s issues of his publication, *The Gardener's Magazine*. One of the American gardening magazines, *The Gardener's Monthly*, printed instructions for creating a basket flower bed in the July 1861 issue.[15] *The Gardener's Monthly* also used an illustration of a woven basket of flowers throughout its publication (see figure 9), which is a recurring motif in the Album quilt in plate 11.

The improvement of cast iron in the mid–nineteenth century provided the material for an extensive supply of outdoor urns and vases. These were placed around the lawn and were filled with a variety of flowers. Illustrations of urns in garden magazines, such as the line drawings found in the January 1835 issue of *The Gardener's Magazine*, could have provided excellent patterns for quiltmakers.[16] (See figures 10A and 10B.) For example, the shapes of the urns seen in the Pots of Flowers quilts (plates 25 and 26) echo the shape of the urns in the magazine illustrations.

Like outdoor basket flower beds, cut flower arrangements incorporated a variety of flowers in each basket or vase. While authors wrote less often about cut-flower arrangements

2

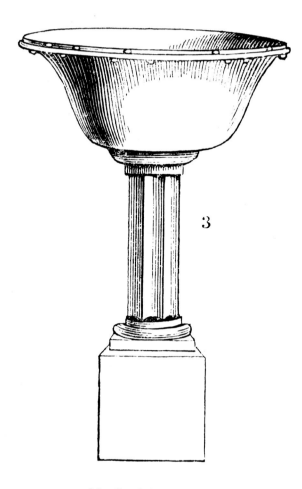

3

than outdoor flower beds, a few authors included sections about flower arranging in their gardening books. Joseph Breck, a Boston horticulturist, included a short chapter titled "The Art of Constructing Bouquets; Arranging Flowers in Vases, Etc." in his 1866 publication, *New Book of Flowers*. In that chapter Breck reprinted hints gleaned from a London newspaper article, "Flowers and Foreign Flower Fashions," an account of an unnamed gentleman's trip to Paris. The writer explained that it was rare to see an arrangement of one variety or even of only one color. The style was to allow each flower to be seen prominently on long stems amid greenery. Never was a vase or urn crowded with

flowers.[17] The arrangement of the floral shapes seen in the Baskets of Flowers quilt (plate 29) and the Baltimore Album-Style quilt (plate 8) exemplifies Breck's commentary.

Another parallel design is found in the borders of many nineteenth-century quilts and the borders outlining the pages of several nineteenth-century publications, including *Godey's Lady's Book and Magazine* and *The Gardener's Monthly*. Frequently used both for the ornamental pages of these publications and in quilts of this period is a serpentine floral-and-vine border like that seen in the Floral Appliqué quilt (plate 30). The intertwining vines that decorate the title pages of

Fig. 11. Title page displaying the decorative vine border used in each issue of *The Gardener's Monthly* in 1859.

the 1859 issues of *The Gardener's Monthly* (see figure 11) are often found in quilt borders of the period as well; see, for example, the Pots of Flowers quilt (plate 25).

The last quarter of the nineteenth century witnessed a dramatic change in the preferred design aesthetics of both gardening and quiltmaking. Gardeners and quiltmakers grew to favor naturalistic, asymmetrical formats over formal, symmetrical arrangements. Many scholars attribute the impetus for this change to the Japanese exhibit at the 1876 Centennial Exhibition.[18] Interest in the exotic art was enhanced by America's fascination with Japanese philosophy. Western social critics and interior designers promoted Japanese decorative arts by arguing that Japanese art embodied ideals similar to those of the West and that Japanese art would, therefore, enhance a Christian home. Proponents of the Japanese style believed that the positive attitude of the worker and the high degree of artisanship resulted in a "sincere" object that would create a proper home environment. This supported the nineteenth-century belief that a woman could influence her family's moral development through her home's furnishings. An unsigned article in an 1880 issue of *Harper's Bazar* stated that the love of beauty was the sign of a "refined mind."[19] Therefore, a woman could be assured that she was doing her utmost to nurture her family by incorporating beautiful designs, such as those in the Japanese style, into her home.

Similarly, crazy quilts rose in popularity during the late nineteenth century because of society's belief that a family's education, culture, and economic position could be discerned through a woman's choice of decorating style. Displaying the family's artistic possessions and decorating the home in good taste were important domestic activities. Additionally,

an object created by the woman herself (such as a crazy quilt) was believed to fulfill several important criteria. First, it was intellectually stimulating for the woman who produced the object and educational for her children to observe her work. Second, the finished object, if made with the correct intentions, would create a "sincere" object of beauty. And third, if displayed in a public part of the home, the quilt would show visitors her high level of culture and skill.[20] Most crazy quilts were made to be showpieces rather than utilitarian items; they were more often seen draped across tables or sofas and found on beds less frequently than the cut-out chintz, album, floral appliqué, and pieced quilts of the first three quarters of the nineteenth century.

The influence of the Japanese style can be seen in the asymmetrical, randomly sized pieces of the popular crazy quilts and the realistically rendered floral and insect embellishments used to decorate their surfaces. The haphazard forms and realistically portrayed flowers of the crazy quilts are a sharp contrast to the symmetrical formats and the fanciful floral motifs used in the pieced and appliquéd quilts created earlier in the century. For example, album quilts and red-and-green floral appliqué quilts of the mid-nineteenth century do not represent the different types of plants and flowers with nearly as much accuracy. They frequently contain floral motifs that mix different species of blooms and leaves or even different petals and leaves on the same plant. See, for example, the Baskets of Flowers quilt (plate 29) or the Floral Appliqué with Eagles quilt (plate 33), which uses eagles as the center of each flower. In addition, the designers of floral appliqué quilts and pieced quilts often stylized the floral motifs to such an extent that the species are not easily identifiable today.[21] This is the case in the Carolina Lily quilt (plate 45), where the technique of piecing dictated the final shape of the flower. Crazy quilts, in contrast, typically embody the Japanese style of realistically portrayed flowers and insects. (See, for example, plates 50 and 52.) Embellishments, which were painted on or embroidered with silk thread or ribbon, allowed finer detail and realism in the crazy quilt than earlier appliqué or geometric piecing techniques using pieces of fabric.

In American gardening in the last quarter of the nineteenth century, the design trend similarly moved away from the symmetrical, geometric style into a new, wild, natural garden design. In this format, tender foreign plants fell out of use in favor of hardy native plants. Native flowers were planted in groupings and allowed to grow into whatever natural drift they chose. American garden writer Peter Henderson advocated a garden design in which single specimens of brilliantly colored flowers were planted in the lawn.[22] This style is similar to the embellishment of crazy quilts, which typically had one floral embellishment on each quilt block; see, for example, the Crazy Quilt with Scripture (plate 51) and the Crazy Quilt in plate 50.

Just as the popular press began calling for the end of the crazy quilt fad by the turn of the century, garden designers began advocating a return to more formal, controlled gardens. Novelist and gardener Edith Wharton launched a campaign to redesign both American home interiors and gardens. She despised the Victorian excess in decorating and gardening and advocated a return to classical, minimalist designs.[23] But the popularity of both crazy quilts and naturalistic gardens endured into the twentieth century.

*

The prominence of flowers in nineteenth-century American culture is summed up in a poem by Harland Coultas published in *Godey's Lady's Book and Magazine* in 1861:

> Blessed be God for flowers,
> For the bright, gentle, holy thoughts that
>   breathe
> From out their odorous beauty like a wreath
> Of sunshine on life's hours.[24]

Flowers provided the basis for spiritual and intellectual improvement. They were believed to possess inherent beauty and sophistication. Scientists, theologians, and popular writers extolled the virtues of women who understood floriculture and incorporated floral designs into their home décor. Furthermore, nineteenth-century women were provided with ample sources of floral and gardening information from which to draw inspiration for their quilt designs. From gardening publications to ladies' magazines, articles regularly appeared that offered designs and patterns suitable for the quiltmakers' use, and editorials encouraged women to engage in gardening. As a result, many women embraced the study of plants and the art and practice of gardening as the basis for spiritual and intellectual improvement. It is also evident from the number of surviving nineteenth-century quilts with floral themes that many women chose to demonstrate their cultivated taste and needlework skills through quiltmaking. Nineteenth-century floral quilts offer us not only a beautiful tradition of women's art, but also a glimpse of the way in which women incorporated society's values and aesthetic preferences into their handiwork.

NOTES

1. J. F. A. Adams, "Is Botany a Suitable Study for Young Men?" *Science*, 4 (Feb. 1887): 116–17.

2. Ann Leighton, *American Gardens of the Nineteenth Century* (Amherst: University of Massachusetts Press, 1987), 316.

3. Walter Elder, *The Cottage Garden of America* (Philadelphia: Moss & Brother, 1848), 13.

4. William H. Adams, *Nature Perfected: Gardens through History* (New York: Abbeville, 1991), 290.

5. Andrew J. Downing, *Cottage Residences* (New York: Wiley & Putnam, 1842), vii.

6. Leighton, *American Gardens*, 68.

7. N. Cleaveland, *The Flowers Personified, being a translation of "Les Fleurs Animées"* (New York: R. Martin, 1847), 76–83.

8. Review of *The Flowers Personified*, by N. Cleaveland, *The Horticulturist and Journal of Rural Art and Rural Taste* 2 (Mar. 1848): 431.

9. Harland Coultas, "Flowers, and What May Be Learned from Them," *Godey's Lady's Book and Magazine*, June 1861, 505.

10. Barbara Rothermel, "Mourning the Children," *Folk Art* (winter 1997–98): 63.

11. Gloria Seaman Allen, curator, DAR Museum, as cited in Ellen F. Eanes et al., *North Carolina Quilts* (Chapel Hill: University of North Carolina Press, 1988), 39.

12. R. R. Reinagle, "Original Beauty of Lines and Forms," *The Gardener's Magazine*, Nov. 1827, 248.

13. Reinagle, "Original Beauty of Lines and Forms," 248–50.

14. Review of *A Treatise on the Theory and Practice of Landscape Gardening*, by A. J. Downing, *The Gardener's Magazine*, Sept. 1841, 472–73.

15. Thomas Meehan, "Garden Decorations," *The Gardener's Monthly*, July 1861, 235.

16. Andrew Patrick, "Descriptive Notice of Some of the Rustic Flower Baskets in the Grounds at Stoke Place," *The Gardener's Magazine*, Jan. 1835, 12–13.

17. Joseph Breck, *New Book of Flowers* (New York: O. Judd, Co., 1866), 47–48.

18. Jane Converse Brown, " 'Fine Arts and Fine People': The Japanese Taste in the American Home, 1876–1916," in *Making the American Home: Middle-Class Women and Domestic Material Culture, 1840–1940*, ed. Marilyn Ferris Motz and Pat Browne (Bowling Green: Bowling Green State University Popular Press, 1988), 121–22; Wendy Kaplan, *"The Art That Is Life": The Arts and Crafts Movement in America, 1875–1920* (Boston: Little, Brown and Company, 1987), 150; Charlotte Gere and Michael Whiteway, *Nineteenth-Century Design: From Pugin to Mackintosh* (New York: Harry N. Abrams, 1994), 158.

19. "Painting on Silk," *Harper's Bazar*, 11 Dec. 1880, 790.

20. Brown, "Fine Arts and Fine People," 136.

21. Dr. Margaret Bolick, curator of botany, and Linda Rader, collections manager of botany, University of Nebraska State Museum, personal communication, 1997–98.

22. Peter Henderson, *Gardening for Pleasure* (New York: Orange Judd Co., 1887), 36.

23. Edith Wharton, *Italian Villas and Their Gardens* (New York: Century Co., 1904), 11.

24. Harland Coultas, "Flowers, and What May Be Learned from Them," *Godey's Lady's Book and Magazine*, June 1861, 505.

FANCIFUL FLOWERS
Botany and the American Quilt

Catalog descriptions by Carolyn Ducey

Plate 1

CENTER MEDALLION WITH CUT-OUT CHINTZ APPLIQUÉ

As in many early-nineteenth-century American quilts, this cut-out chintz appliqué quilt has a central focus or medallion format. In its center, an extravagant floral arrangement flourishes in a wicker basket that is placed within a stylized garden fence. Both the basket and the graceful urns of flowers in the body of the quilt display a mix of red roses, peonies, dahlias, and cornflowers that create a stunning visual image. Butterflies and birds fly among the abundant blooms. A dominant red inner border surrounds the center motif, while a similar oversized swag encloses the whole of the quiltmaker's teeming chintz garden. The entire quilt is at last framed within a glossy chintz border that incorporates a variety of flowers. The chintz fabric still retains its sleek shine, produced by applying a beeswax solution to the fabric and then polishing it with an agate stone or some other suitable material.[1]

Chintz was originally imported to Europe from India in the seventeenth century for use in home furnishings. It became very popular, undercutting the wool and silk markets that had previously been unchallenged for use in household furnishings and clothing. Despite initial opposition from textile producers, the cotton market continued to expand. In the eighteenth century, French and English manufacturers learned the printing and dyeing techniques of the Indian printed and painted cottons and initiated production of similar fabrics in Europe. Late in the eighteenth century, America also developed the spinning, weaving, and printing technology for the mass production of cotton fabrics.

Cut-out chintz quilts may also be called *broderie perse* quilts. The term refers to a style of Persian embroidery that cut-out chintz quilts are thought to resemble. Although *broderie perse* is believed to be a recent name for this style of quilt, it is interesting to note that nineteenth-century gardeners and writers used a related term, *parterre de broderie*, to describe a particular type of garden.[2] The *parterre de broderie* garden is a French garden style wherein serpentine flower beds are cut into large expanses of lawn. In both quilts and gardens, the *broderie* designs incorporate groups of flowers on a neutral background to evoke images of embroidered textiles.

The fabric used for the back of this quilt still retains the manufacturer's stamps. One reads "Lowell Bleachery Finish," identifying a textile mill in Lowell, Massachusetts, that became one of America's most important centers of textile production in the second quarter of the nineteenth century. An eagle with outstretched wings hovering over a curved garland frames the manufacturer's name. Another stamp identifies the type of cloth that was used for the quilt's back. As with the previous stamp, the words "Superfine Long Cloth" are framed by a swirling floral garland. Within the garland stands a large urn. A third stamp is simply a bouquet of various buds, flowers, and leaves. These stamps would most likely have disappeared with frequent laundering.

NOTES

The abbreviation QSPI in the catalog entries stands for "quilt stitches per inch."

1. Jeremy Adamson, *Calico and Chintz: Antique Quilts from the Collection of Patricia S. Smith* (Washington DC: Smithsonian Institution, Renwick Gallery, 1997), 23.

2. Gloria Seaman Allen, curator, DAR Museum, as cited in Ellen F. Eanes et al., *North Carolina Quilts* (Chapel Hill: University of North Carolina Press, 1988), 39.

QUILTMAKER:
Unknown

ORIGIN:
Possibly New England, c. 1830–50

Cotton

QSPI 7

113" x 115"

1997.007.454

Plate 2

STAR OF BETHLEHEM WITH CUT-OUT CHINTZ APPLIQUÉ

This star of Bethlehem quilt is exceptionally large, measuring nearly nine feet on each side. The size reflects the practice of making very large quilts during the first half of the nineteenth century. An oversize quilt was needed to accommodate the large beds, which in wealthy households were piled high with feather mattresses or ticks. Later in the century, when an increasing number of middle-class women undertook quiltmaking, most quilts became smaller in size, presumably because smaller beds were used in their more modest homes.

The bright blue, yellow, and pink of the calico fabrics that make up the striking star pattern of this quilt are repeated in the many sprays of chintz flowers that surround it. Different species of exotic flowers are combined on a single stem, illustrating how quiltmakers often sought to create striking visual effects rather than realistic representations of plants. For example, in the sprays in the bottom corners of the quilt delicate bluebells, lilacs, and tulips bloom together.

Quilt historians and collectors have documented star quilts that incorporate chintz cut-out designs in Maryland, Virginia, North Carolina, and South Carolina, leading them to conclude that these quilts were made primarily in the southeastern region of the United States.[1] This quilt was acquired in Pennsylvania according to the dealer; no other provenance is available.

The extremely thin batting often used in quilts made in the South helped the quiltmaker in her effort to sew tiny, even quilting stitches. Her stitches create a grid pattern in the center of the quilt that contrasts with the diagonal lines quilted in the outer border.

NOTE

1. Amelia Peck, *American Quilts & Coverlets in the Metropolitan Museum of Art* (New York: Metropolitan Museum of Art and Dutton Studio Books, 1990), 31.

QUILTMAKER:
Unknown

ORIGIN:
Probably southeastern United States, c. 1830–50

Cotton

QSPI 12

104″ x 104″

1997.007.369

Plate 3
CENTER MEDALLION WITH CUT-OUT CHINTZ APPLIQUÉ

Cut-out chintz quilts were the show quilts of the 1840s, in part due to the extraordinary chintz fabrics that were used to create them. This quilt incorporates numerous floral chintz-fabric motifs as well as an unusual center panel. The center block depicts Queen Victoria, wearing a rich red gown, as she stands on a balcony surrounded by oversized flowers. An overflowing urn engraved with the initials "V. R." (Victoria Regina) is placed to her left and a pedestal supporting a reclining lion to the right. Around the center block, a variety of appliquéd flowers and wreaths thrive.

Although this quilt was most likely made in America (the provenance is unknown), some of the fabrics may be English. The fabric of the outer border of the quilt, a glowing chintz whose vines and flowers undulate gracefully, can also be found in a star of Bethlehem quilt in the collection of the Metropolitan Museum of Art.[1] Amelia Peck, associate curator in the Department of American Decorative Arts at the Metropolitan Museum, identifies the fabric as English in origin. This quiltmaker used the fabric both as a distinctive frame for the varied blocks of her quilt and for its binding.

The artfully arranged flowers and wreaths of the quilt are similar to the *parterre de broderie* garden style, popular in the nineteenth century (see cat. 1). The quiltmaker quilted floral patterns in each corner of the individual blocks. The space left between the floral motifs is filled with echo quilting. A tiny woven basket is quilted within the wreath featured below and to the right of the center panel. The border is quilted with a double diagonal line.

Five of the quilt's blocks are signed in ink (see chart).

NOTE

1. Amelia Peck, *American Quilts & Coverlets in the Metropolitan Museum of Art* (New York: Metropolitan Museum of Art and Dutton Studio Books, 1990), 31 (illus. no. 7, accession no. 1973.204).

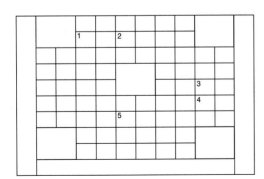

INSCRIPTIONS:

1. William Rogers Surgeon, Born April 26, 1843

2. Josephine Craig, 1844

3. Elizabeth Schaffer, Aug. 1844

4. Helen Craig, 1844

5. Debby Schaffer, Aug. 1844

QUILTMAKER:
Includes multiple signatures

ORIGIN:
Probably United States, dated 1843 and 1844

Cotton

QSPI 11

92.5" x 109.5"

1997.007.479

Plate 4
CUT-OUT CHINTZ APPLIQUÉ

A close look at the extravagant chintz flower bouquets placed around the entire border of this quilt reveals the maker's economical use of fabric: three separate pieces of fabric are sewn together to create a complete bouquet. The diamonds of the star pattern and the delicate grace of the soft blue, reverse-appliquéd plumes offset the rich floral imagery. The whole quilt is framed in a chintz fabric that features brightly colored flowers.

The maker also incorporated outstanding design elements in the quilt. At the four corners of the central square, identical stars punctuate the plumes running between them. A rhythmic green swag drapes from the eight extended points of the center star, and small appliquéd half circles form a square that frames the quilt's center. Within the square, delicate cut-out chintz flowers blossom.

A great variety of quilting patterns are included in the quilt's overall design. Linear outline quilting is used in the diamond shapes of the center star. Echo quilting fills the spaces around the gentle swags, and quilted leaves are sprinkled between the stars. The maker quilted both a simple diagonal line and a diagonal grid between the floral baskets, which are first highlighted with outline quilting.

The base of the floral baskets may be the top, or capital, of a cut-out chintz column. Columnar designs, often called "pillar prints," were popular on printed chintz after 1825. Though the style quickly faded, the fabric can be found on quilts throughout the 1840s and 1850s. Again, as with the pieced floral bouquets, the quiltmaker demonstrated an ingenious method of using her valuable fabrics.

QUILTMAKER:
Unknown

ORIGIN:
Possibly New England, c. 1830–50

Cotton

QSPI 9

108" x 100"

1997.007.659

Plate 5
ALBUM

This quiltmaker used an interesting combination of stylized patterns and cut-out chintz designs to create her album quilt. The chintz fabric includes both floral imagery and exotic figural images. For example, in a block in the top row, musicians lead a man riding an elephant, seated in an elaborate howdah, or covered saddle. In the same row, figures traverse a path under the swaying fronds of a palm tree. In the bottom row, escorts playing cymbals and a triangle accompany a man riding a stately camel.

These unusual designs illustrate the fascination that exotic Asian cultures held for the Western world of the eighteenth and nineteenth centuries. Merchant trade sparked an interest in China in the seventeenth century that brought porcelain, lacquer, silk, and ivory to the West. The exotic items became very popular, and in response to consumers' demands, European manufacturers began to produce merchandise whose design forms reflected a romanticized image of the East. The use of this Oriental style, referred to as *chinoiserie*, was found in furniture, textiles, interior design, and garden design. Asymmetrical forms, Oriental figures, and lacquering and gilding are characteristics of the *chinoiserie* style.

This quilt illustrates properties of the English *gardenesque*-style garden, which became popular in America during the middle of the nineteenth century. In this style, described by A. J. Downing in his 1841 book, *A Treatise on the Theory and Practice of Landscape Gardening, Adapted to North America*, each tree and flower bed must be able to stand alone on its artistic merit yet still be able to be integrated into a larger design plan. The object, according to excerpts of Downing's book published in *The Gardener's Magazine*, was to produce "highly elegant and polished forms."[1] The individual floral motifs on separate blocks combine to create an elegant quilt.

Cut-out chintz floral sprays and calico fabrics cut into botanically inspired shapes are applied to the white background of the quilt with a delicate whipstitch. The chain border is one piece of fabric appliquéd to extend the length of each side of the quilt. The designs are highlighted by a simple gridwork of quilting stitches. Faint blue lines remain where the quilter marked her quilting lines, suggesting that the quilt has never been washed.

NOTE

1. Review of *A Treatise on the Theory and Practice of Landscape Gardening*, by A. J. Downing, *The Gardener's Magazine*, Sept. 1841, 472–73.

QUILTMAKER:
Unknown

ORIGIN:
Possibly Pennsylvania, c. 1830–60

Cotton

QSPI 8

98" x 97"

1997.007.890

Plate 6
SIGNATURE ALBUM QUILT TOP

Mary Van Pelt, for whom this album quilt top was made, may have been leaving on a long journey—perhaps migrating from Maryland to a western state. Many of the blocks on her quilt top, signed by friends and relatives (see chart), reflect a melancholy sadness. In fact, the evocative content of the ink-inscribed messages suggest another possible impetus for making this quilt—Mary's untimely death. For example, one inscription reads, "My dear, lie in slumber. Holy angels guard thy bed." Mary's sister, J. H. Van Pelt, inscribed a personal message on one of the blocks:

> My sister, my sweet sister
> . . . No tears but tenderness to answer mine
> Go where I will to me thou art the same
> A loved regret which I would not resign.

Album quilts, most popular in the United States in the mid–nineteenth century, generally consisted of appliquéd motifs and were made both by individuals and by groups. Friendship album quilts sometimes were given as tokens of remembrance to family and friends leaving for the West. Presentation album quilts were given as gifts to ministers, teachers, and public figures. Memorial album quilts and mourning quilts, though rare compared to friendship album quilts, were sometimes made. Although we will never know with certainty whether this was intended to be a friendship or memorial album quilt, a number of the quilt top's signed blocks provide clues to its place of origin. The inscriptions on three blocks include "Havre de Grace," a town located in Maryland on the Chesapeake Bay, thirty miles northeast of Baltimore.

The finely executed botanical images used on Mary's quilt top may have sentimental symbolism: roses and tulips may declare love, oak leaves represent strength, and daisies sometimes symbolize farewell. The practice of attaching symbolic meaning to flowers developed into a widely accepted "language of flowers" in the United States during the nineteenth century. Understanding the symbolic meaning of flowers was thought to show a person's culture and social standing.

INKED INSCRIPTIONS:

1. Forget me not, don't forget me. O. A. Bills, M[a]y 26, 1849

2. Mrs. Chew, Havre de Grace, Md.

3. [First line illegible] . . . the recollection of one [illegible word] brek, hath more in it to tranquilize you, The darkness of despondency than of gayety and pleasure. Paula [illegible last name]

4. Fanny Kent

5. H. M. Boyd [Royal], Havre de Grace, Md., 1849

6. Gertrude E. Jackson

7. Pauline Cheer [?], Havre de Grace, Md., 1849

8. Eliza Ann Ebbets [?], Octobe[r] 4th, [18]49

9. Emma Van Pelt, April [18]50

10. My sister! My sweet sister! You name [illegible word]. Dearer and purer were it. Should be these mountains and seas divide us, but I claim no tears but tenderness to answer mine. Go where I will to me, thou art the same, a loved regret which I would not resign. J. H. Van Pelt [18]49

11. Hey Diddle Diddle

12. Ann Van Pelt, May [18]49, my mother dear

13. Emma Lawdon, April [18]50

14. To Mary: "May Heaven its blessings on thee find, / And loves pure flame thy soul inspire; / In friendships bright and lasting chain / Received every fond desire. / Goodnight, yet o're thy peaceful dreams [?], / May angels guard the while, / And when thou wak'st with joy and [illegible word], / As faithful o're thee smile." Jane [illegible word] Ebbets, 1849

15. Amelia Grey

16. Hush! my dear, lie still in slumber. Holy angels guard thy bed.

17. Mrs. Lawson

18. Emilie Husted, July 1854

19. The early bird which in the sun unfold with May dew overrun [?], are likest thee, when I would throw loves warmth upon me long ago. C. Bills, Aug 1849.

20. Anna C. Husted

21. Eliza Browes

22. Mary [illegible word] Collier, [illegible word] [18] 49

23. Martha[?] Kent

24. Maria Bullis[?]

25. Emma Van Pelt, April [18]50

26. C. V. P. [embroidered]

27. If six or sixty prayers are past, a blessing surely comes at last. Pray on and never faint to cheer a drooping saint. Adaline Smith, June 1849

28. Cornelia Van Pelt, April [18]50

29. Jane

30. Euphemia Warren, May 30, [illegible date]

31. H. H. S. [embroidered, cross-stitch]

32. [Illegible]

33. E. L. [embroidered]

1	2		3	4	5	6
7		8				9
		10	11	12		13
	14	15			16	17
		18	19	20		21
	22			23	24	25
26	27	28	29			
	30		31	32	33	

QUILTMAKER:
Includes various signatures

ORIGIN:
Maryland, dated 1849, 1850, 1854

Cotton

No quilting

94" x 84.5"

1997.007.654

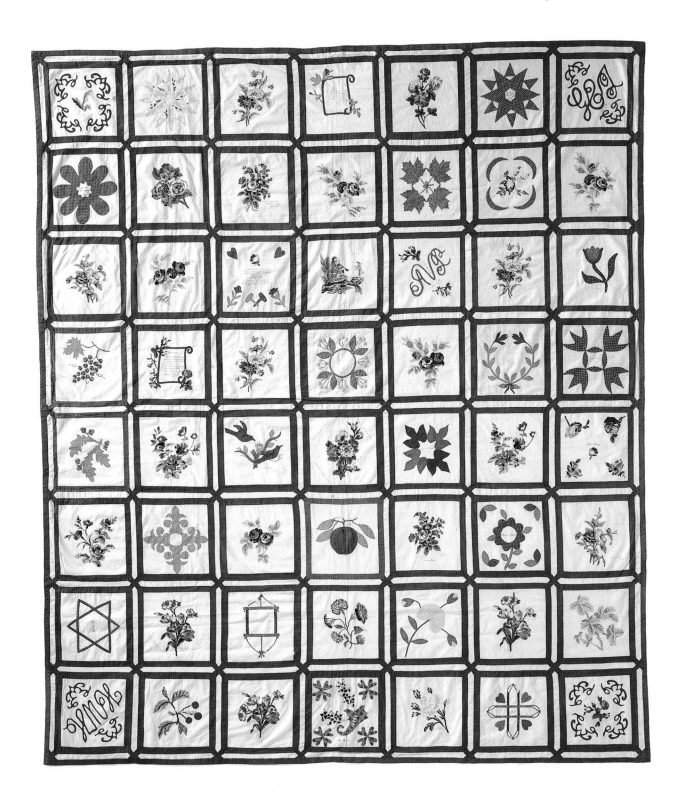

Plate 7

BALTIMORE ALBUM

Baltimore album quilts have a unique history in American quilting. Quilt historians believe the quilts were made during the 1840s and 1850s in Baltimore, Maryland. They are very distinct in their designs and elaborate needlework. In fact, many of the floral designs of the Baltimore albums are similar to those seen in early chintz fabrics, leading some textile historians to suggest that the makers of album quilts were attempting to emulate the expensive chintz fabrics.[1]

Among the intricate floral designs of this quilt's twenty-five appliquéd blocks are black-eyed Susans, blue forget-me-nots, tulips, a white flowering French lilac, and a morning glory wreath. In addition, layered fabrics create a clipper ship, sailing with the American flag proudly blowing in the sea breeze, and an apple or cherry tree, complete with an egg-filled nest. Baskets and cornucopias overflow with their garden bounty. Fine quilting stitches create a diagonal grid over the entire quilt's surface.

By the early 1800s cotton had grown in popularity for use in clothing and household textiles in both the United States and Europe. The production of cotton goods became widespread and cotton fabric more available. In fact, Baltimore was home to a number of textile mills, giving local women a wide range of cotton prints for quilting. Baltimore's location as a seaport also increased the availability of cotton from England and France.

A similar Baltimore album quilt, with a number of nearly identical blocks and fabrics, is located in the collection of the Maryland Historical Society.[2] The resemblance of designs found in the two quilts suggests that they were based on a common pattern or made by the same designer. Jennifer Goldsborough, author of *Lavish Legacies*, a catalog of the Baltimore album quilts in the Maryland Historical Society's collection, describes styles and fabrics that are consistent in a number of the individual block patterns of quilts in their collection. Goldsborough hypothesizes that a Mrs. Simon may have been the individual responsible for designing the similar blocks in a large number of Baltimore album quilts. Goldsborough found an 1850 diary notation of Hannah M. Trimble that describes two quilts and identifies Mary Simon as the "lady who cut and basted these handsome quilts."[3]

NOTES

1. Jennifer Goldsborough, *Lavish Legacies: Baltimore Albums and Related Quilts in the Collection of the Maryland Historical Society* (Baltimore: Maryland Historical Society, 1994), 10.
2. Goldsborough, *Lavish Legacies*, 60–61.
3. Goldsborough, *Lavish Legacies*, 16–17.

QUILTMAKER:
Unknown

ORIGIN:
Probably Baltimore, Maryland, c. 1845–55

Cotton, silk, linen

QSPI 11

110″ x 104″

1997.007.320

Plate 8
BALTIMORE ALBUM STYLE

The blocks of this quilt contain a great variety of patterns. Elaborate baskets filled with flowers and vines are placed next to bold stars and wreaths. Other blocks contain highly stylized floral patterns. The double-sawtooth border highlights a complex red-and-green tulip vine that surrounds the album blocks.

This is a fine example of the album quilt style that was popular in the mid–nineteenth century. It appears to have been constructed by a single person, as indicated by the even appliqué and quilting stitches. Many of the pattern blocks are simplified: the elaborate fabric layering in multiple colors associated with Baltimore albums is not found in this quilt. Simple floral wreaths, composed solely of red-and-green-colored fabrics, illustrate the trend away from elaborately stitched and layered handwork to a more simplified design. A large crewel-like embroidered wool star in the bottom row is as unusual as the silk-embroidered star directly above it.

The quilt is covered with a variety of quilting designs. A number of blocks have elaborate floral patterns in the white space around the designs. Echo quilting is also used to accent the array of patterns.

QUILTMAKER:
Unknown

ORIGIN:
Possibly Baltimore, Maryland, c. 1850–60

Cotton, wool, silk

QSPI 11

96″ x 96″

1997.007.300

Plate 9

SIGNATURE ALBUM

Flags, flowers, and fruit grace this striking album quilt amid pieced quilt blocks that include stars, triangles, and baskets. Stuffed berries flourish on a circular wreath; cut-out chintz flowers fill four baskets placed in the corners of the quilt; and four flags are proudly displayed. The American flag, with thirteen stars, is easy to recognize. The other flags represent Great Britain, Sweden, and France.

Signatures, locations, and dates are signed in ink on the quilt and offer tantalizing clues to its origin and purpose (see chart). The Stiles and Higgins families of Elizabethtown, New York,[1] and the Stokes family from Philadelphia each have a number of family members' names on the various quilt blocks. Most blocks are simply dated with either 1851 or 1852, but seven contain specific dates: April 18, 1852; June 1 and June 23, 1851; and two duplicated dates, July 4, 1851, and March 25, 1851. Some blocks include delicate imagery framing the signed name: a lyre, floral wreath, and detailed leaves, for example. The names may represent the makers of the different blocks; the different skill levels of appliqué stitching and the variety in size of the quilting stitches suggest that different makers were involved in the blocks' construction. Perhaps further research can reveal the connections among these families' names.

A number of unusual embellishments created with ribbon or fabric tape add interest to this quilt: a woven basket (bottom row), a series of paisley motifs framed by an intricate chain border (left edge), a wreath that holds cherries (center), and the ivy vine (center right). Embroidered details also add to the quilt's interest. A floral pattern, delicately chain stitched in red floss, is surrounded by looping, intertwining vines, stitched in a double line. The top of each flagpole is highlighted with a gold button.

NOTE

1. We assume that the "Elizabethtown" inscribed on so many of the blocks made by members of the Higgins family refers to Elizabethtown, New York, since Margaret Higgins simply listed New York on her block. However, there is an Elizabethtown, Pennsylvania, which is located about ninety miles west of Philadelphia.

INSCRIPTIONS:

1. Sarah H. Bolton

2. Susan H. Higgins, Elizabethtown, 1851

3. Mary Ann [illegible]

4. Charlotte P. Higgins, Elizabeth-town, 1851

5. Martha Renaud[?], Elizabethtown, 1852

6. John Stiles, Elizabethtown, 1852

7. Josephine A. Stokes, Philadelphia, March 25th, 1851

8. Elizabeth L. [illegible]

9. Susan M. Stiles, Elizabethtown, 1852

10. Margaret A. Higgins, New York, 1852

11. Mary Augustine

12. Hannah Stiles, Elizabethtown, 1852

13. Charles Augustine, Philadelphia, 1851

14. Abigail W. Stokes, 1851

15. Abby J.[?] Kettlewell[?]

16. Mary E. Stiles, Elizabethtown, 1851

17. Mary Stiles, 1852, Elizabethtown

18. Cornelia Stokes

19. Margaret Higgins, Newark, 1852

20. C. Eugene Stokes, Philadelphia, 1851

21. Cornelia J.[?] Yates [Gates], Elizabethtown, 1852

22. Charles Stokes, Philadelphia, 1851

23. U. W. Stokes

24. Sarah Albright, Phila., 1851

25. A. E. Nekervis

26. May A. Peckworth, Phila., 1851

27. Howard Lamartine Stokes, July 4th, 1851

28. Wm. Yates [Gates], Elizabethtown, 1852

29. Josephine A. Stokes, Philadelphia, 1852

30. H. Yates [Gates], Elizabethtown, 1852

31. Eliza B. Day, Elizabeth [illegible], April 18th, 1852

32. C. A. Taylor, June 23, 1851, Phila.

33. Cornelia T. Yates [Gates]

34. Granville Stokes

35. William L. [?] Augustine

36. William Jerard [?] Stokes, July 4th, 1851

37. L. H. Higgins, Elizabethtown, 1852

38. Wm. B. Higgins, Newark, 1851

39. Lydia Taylor, Phila., 1851

40. William Stiles, 1852, Elizabeth-town

41. S. H. Nekervis

42. Mary A. Higgerd

43. J. C. Yohe

44. Jane E. Crane, 1852, Elizabeth-town

45. G. E. Taylor, June 23rd, 1851, Phila.

46. Mary Hammitt, West Elizabeth, 1851

47. Susan H. Higgins

48. A. S. Stokes

49. Sarah Albright, Philadelphia, March 25th, 1851

50. Rebecca R. Hibberd, Philadelphia, June 1st, 1851

51. Louisa Stiles

52. Julia A. Taylor, Phila., 1851

53. Lewis Augustine

54. Maria Louisa Elden, Phila., 1851

55. Phebe C. Higgins, Elizabethtown, 1852

56. Sarah Boyd

1	2	3	4	5	6	7	8
9	10	11	12	13	14	15	16
17	18	19	20	21	22	23	24
25	26	27	28	29	30	31	32
33	34	35	36	37	38	39	40
41	42	43	44	45	46	47	48
49	50	51	52	53	54	55	56

QUILTMAKER:
Includes various signatures

ORIGIN:
Signature locations include Elizabethtown NY[?]; Philadelphia PA; Newark NJ; West Elizabeth NJ[?]; New York; dated 1851 and 1852

Cotton

QSPI 7

96" x 110"

1997.007.666

Plate 10
ALBUM

In the center of this quilt an orange tree holds abundant fruit. It is surrounded by a variety of lush botanical motifs, expertly sewn to the quilt. The maker stitched one particularly unusual block, which is found in the bottom row; it comprises a series of concentric rings around a circle, with a moon, star, and planets placed in the block's corners. The maker also added patriotic elements, including two blocks with American flags. One flag has thirteen stars, perhaps representing the original thirteen colonies; the other has none. Another patriotic design can be found in the square below the orange tree, which holds thirteen red stars. The initials M. H. are stitched near the center of the quilt.

While most of the designs are attached with a nearly invisible whipstitch, a number are further embellished with a delicate feather stitch. For example, the basket below and to the right of the orange tree has embroidery over all of its green fabric, creating a wicker-like appearance. Feather stitches also anchor the edges of the oranges growing on the center tree. The maker used a cut-out chintz technique in a block in the bottom row that is filled with sprays of roses. The delicacy and precision of the needlework suggests that it is the work of one person.

The use of an orange tree in the center of the quilt is unusual. However, citrus fruits like oranges and lemons were very popular in Europe and America in the nineteenth century. The first information about raising citrus fruits spread as the Roman Empire expanded and as merchant traffic along Arab trade routes increased. During the sixteenth century, the cultivation of fruit trees became popular in Europe.

A fugitive green dye, probably a synthetic, has been used in this quilt, leaving behind a drab tan in its place. An English scientist developed the first synthetic dye in 1856; other synthetic dyes soon followed and offered quilters a new color palette. Colorfast green dyes, however, proved to be especially difficult to produce; consequently, many of the green elements in quilts of the last half of the nineteenth century have faded, leaving behind a dreary reminder of the fabrics' former brilliance.

QUILTMAKER:
Unknown

ORIGIN:
Possibly Maryland,
c. 1860–70

Cotton

QSPI 10

95″ x 83″

1997.007.462

Plate 11
ALBUM

This vibrant album quilt overflows with vivid color, textured fabric details, and visual exuberance. Framed by a simple leaf border on two sides and large-scale budding stems in each of the four corners, scattered groupings of cherries, holly, and poppies abound. Numerous berries adorn nearly every floral element of the quilt, and some are stuffed to create a three-dimensional effect. Other berries are fabric "yo-yos"—circles of fabric gathered together to form a ruche effect and then attached to the quilt. Among the profusion of leaves, plants, and berries, the quiltmaker has embroidered birds and flying insects. She has also used embroidery to embellish the many plants in the quilt. These elements add a certain spontaneity to the quilt design and seem to express the quilter's joy in making her quilt.

A number of plants are used in this quilt's design: the Oriental poppy, American holly, cherries, cockscomb, and pansies. These plants thrive throughout the United States. American holly, a symbol of Christmas, grows from Massachusetts south to central Florida and from the West to the East Coast, making it widely available. Pansies have been grown for such a long period of time, in diverse areas and conditions, and with so many different variations, that their origin is unknown.

QUILTMAKER:
Unknown

ORIGIN:
Possibly Pennsyl-
vania, c. 1860–80

Cotton, silk

QSPI 6

68.5″ x 66″

1997.007.440

Plate 12
MARINER'S COMPASS
WITH TULIPS

Simple tulips grow amidst a series of bright circles in this unusual quilt. In the sunburst pattern, found in both the center of the concentric circles and in individual motifs outside the circles, triangles are set around an octagonal center, creating a bold explosion of color. The quiltmaker may have struggled with the piecing of the sunbursts, as indicated by the fabric that she has gathered and "eased in" to make the triangles fit. The circle and sunbursts are contained within a border of contrasting red diamonds and green triangles.

Plumes are repeated in the quilting stitches between the various rings. In the wide, white border, large grape leaves with curling tendrils are quilted in the alternating curves of a slender vine.

The defined lines of the Mariner's Compass pattern are reminiscent of a formal style of gardening that was popular in France during the seventeenth and eighteenth centuries. The style, popularized by French designer André Le Nôtre's designs for the Versailles palace gardens, promoted gardens with elaborate, geometrical beds and numerous fountains, often circular in shape. The style mirrored the symmetry of architecture during the same period. In the latter part of the eighteenth century, a more natural look replaced the formal French style, in part due to the influx of foreign plants into the European market.

QUILTMAKER:
Unknown

ORIGIN:
Probably
Lancaster,
Pennsylvania,
c. 1850–70

Cotton

QSPI 7

95" x 90"

1997.007.909

Plate 13
DOUBLE IRISH CHAIN

A glowing orange rainbow print with a honeycomb ground is used to create a distinctive line that stretches from corner to corner in this Irish chain quilt. A curved floral vine in the outer border contrasts with the linear quality of the pattern's squares.

According to quilt scholar Barbara Brackman, in her book titled *Clues in the Calico*, rainbow fabrics were popular for use in wallpaper and quilts in the mid–nineteenth century. They were the result of a delicate shading of color on the rollers used to print cotton fabrics. The result is a progression of color intensities, passing from light to dark and back to light. Rainbow prints continued to be used in quilts up to 1860 and are found in quilts only occasionally after that date.[1]

A careful look at this quilt reveals exquisite details. In the large areas of white fabric, delicate pineapples, lyres, and wreaths have been quilted and then stuffed with extra batting to appear three-dimensional. In order to create this depth the quiltmaker first stitched an outline of the quilting design in the fabric; then, on the reverse side, she carefully separated the threads of the backing fabric and added extra stuffing. The appliquéd flowers and buds of the outer border also hold extra stuffing, likely added as the fabric pieces were attached to the background fabric. Exceptional mastery of appliqué is demonstrated in the long borders of triangles that are attached to the quilt in a single length of fabric.

The maker of this quilt, Rhoda E. Smith, stitched her name and the year 1853 in a delicate cross-stitch on the quilt's back. Born in Benton, New York, in 1826, Rhoda married a farmer, Oscar Nutt, on 26 June 1854. They had two sons, William and Smith. Rhoda died on 13 March 1911 at the age of eighty-five.[2]

NOTES

1. Barbara Brackman, *Clues in the Calico* (McLean VA: EPM Publications, Inc., 1989), 86.
2. Genealogical research was done by Stacy Epstein, former curator of the Ardis and Robert James Collection. Records are from the Yates County Genealogical and Historical Society, Oliver House Museum, Penn Yan, New York.

QUILTMAKER:
Rhoda E. Smith

ORIGIN:
Benton, New York, dated 1853

Cotton

QSPI 13

100" x 80"

1997.007.665

Plate 14
WHIG ROSE VARIATION

Numerous rose designs are found in quilts of the nineteenth century, with many different names given to the subtle pattern variations. Pattern names also varied between different locations. For example, this pattern was sometimes called Whig rose and at other times democratic rose, named after the two major parties competing for political power in the early nineteenth century. Sometimes the pattern was called the rose of Sharon.

The border on this quilt is dynamic. Large birds appear ready to pluck fruit from the vine that encircles them. Delicate urns with reverse-appliquéd inserts contain stems graced by heart-shaped blooms. Tiny buttonhole stitches add detail to the birds and to the flowers and leaves surrounding them. In addition, carefully cut out white spots are used as the birds' eyes.

Unique motifs are embroidered in dark thread in the white space between the middle and bottom rows of the quilt. On the left, two interlocking hearts are stitched. On the right, a feathered wreath surrounds the initials "E. C.," and in the middle the date 1853 is embroidered inside a quilted sunburst.

Superb quilting between the Whig rose designs includes a detailed eagle holding a banner that reads "E Pluribus Unum," an overflowing urn of flowers, pomegranates, pineapples, bunches of grapes, and assorted flowers. All of the white background is quilted with various figures; any space between them is filled with stipple quilting of lines less than a quarter of an inch apart. These tiny quilting stitches and imaginative quilting designs make this quilt a masterpiece of handwork.

This quilt is nearly identical to another Whig rose featured in the "Fanciful Flowers" exhibit and included in this catalog as plate 15. The appliqué designs appear nearly identical, and the unique borders contain only subtle differences. According to the dealer, this quilt was found in Ohio, whereas the other was found in Indiana. No known connection exists between the two quilts.

QUILTMAKER:
Unknown

ORIGIN:
Possibly Ohio,
dated 1853

Cotton

QSPI 12

88″ x 87″

1997.007.570

Plate 15
WHIG ROSE

A tour de force of appliqué and quilting, this Whig rose quilt incorporates six layers of fabric in the construction of its large, stylized flowers. Carefully balanced with oversized, green leaves, four stems extend outward, gently curving to frame the inner flower of the pattern. A simple rose blooms at the end of the stems.

The border of this quilt is a delicate pattern of birds and vines holding clusters of berries or grapes. Ripe red berries and new green berries grow together; small brown birds hover above each cluster as if ready to pluck the tasty fruit. The red cardinals and alternating yellow and green birds, as well as the small yellow birds that flank the vases in the border, have already feasted on the various fruits—they all hold a yellow berry in their beaks. The flowers, vases, and birds are set among curved, interlocking vines that illustrate the maker's mastery of appliqué technique. Embroidered details are used effectively in outlining the yellow birds; a chain stitch is used for the birds' legs and as contour lines for the large birds.

Grapes and berries are common elements of appliqué quilts. They may symbolize abundance or, as in still-life paintings, represent aging: after maturity or ripeness, death follows. They may also refer to viticulture and the process of making wine. Instructions for winemaking spread throughout the world in the sixteenth and seventeenth centuries as countries were colonized. Spanish missionaries introduced grape cultivation to lower California in the eighteenth century.

The floral imagery of the quilt is repeated in the extraordinary quilting designs that create a textural surface: a surfeit of quilted leaves and vines fill the space between the Whig rose motifs. Double lines of diagonal quilting fill the space that remains.

Note the similarity between this Whig rose quilt found in Indiana and another found in Ohio (see plate 14). Were they made by the same quiltmaker? By two sisters, or by a mother and daughter? No information is available to explain their uncanny resemblance. The Whig rose pattern appears nearly identical in both quilts; the unique borders contain only subtle differences. Similar quilts are known to have been made in Ohio, as well as in Pennsylvania and New York.[1] It is possible that this quilt was made in Ohio and taken with a family to Indiana when they migrated farther west.

NOTE

1. See Ricky Clark, ed., *Quilts in Community: Ohio's Traditions* (Nashville TN: Rutledge Hill, 1991), 23; Jacqueline Atkins and Phyllis Tepper, *New York Beauties: Quilts from the Empire State* (New York: Dutton Studio Books, 1992), 112.

QUILTMAKER:
Unknown

ORIGIN:
Possibly Indiana,
c. 1850–60

Cotton

QSPI 11

92" x 94"

1997.007.718

Plate 16
PRAIRIE ROSE WITH MEDALLION CENTER

The large designs of this quilt incorporate a tree trunk and branches with roselike flowers similar to those used in many rose-pattern variations. The outer border features small, red berries on a trailing vine that has different leaves than those found on the trees in the center of the quilt.

Roses, popular in nineteenth-century quilt designs, are one of the most popular plants in gardening history. They are often featured in both home gardens and botanical gardens. Botanical gardens, whose purpose is to identify and classify plant species and to breed new plants, have been in existence in America for over two hundred and fifty years and remain active today. The oldest, Bartram's Garden in Philadelphia, opened in 1731. The U.S. Botanical Garden opened in Washington DC in 1850, and the Missouri Botanical Garden in St. Louis began operation in 1859. Due in part to the efforts of botanists at gardens like these, hundreds of new roses are available for today's gardeners.

This quiltmaker used two different green fabrics for the leaves and vine in this quilt, both of which were dyed using a two-step process. Prior to the development of synthetic dyes, a two-step dyeing process was frequently used to create green colors because no grass-green dyes exist in nature. Therefore, either a blue dye was used with yellow or a yellow dye was applied over blue to create green colors. The two different green fabrics in this quilt illustrate the result of uneven fading in two-step dyed greens—in the outer border the green fabric now has a yellowish hue where the blue dye faded more readily. In contrast, the stems and leaves of the center design reveal areas where a blue color now dominates, indicating that the yellow dye was less colorfast in this fabric. The quiltmaker, Eliza J. Herron, embroidered her name and the date 1857 on the quilt.

QUILTMAKER:
Eliza J. Herron

ORIGIN:
Probably Pennsylvania, dated 1857

Cotton

QSPI 8

92″ x 92″

1997.007.908

Plate 17
BLOSSOM WREATH

The gently curving vine of this blossom wreath quilt holds trios of bright flowers and large buds. The same composite design is used in the undulating outer border. The flowers feature a striking color combination. Their pistils are a bright yellow. The petals are cut from a vivid Turkey red calico fabric printed with small yellow and blue motifs. The bright red calico fabric is often found in quilts made between 1830 and 1860.[1] The contrast of the bright yellow-and-blue print against the saturated red fabric makes the quilt sparkle.

Linear quilting contrasts with the flowing vines of the appliquéd wreath pattern on this quilt. Plumes created with fine quilting form diagonal lines in the space between the striking appliquéd blossoms; a quilted diagonal grid fills the diamond shapes between the plumes and extends outward to the edges of the quilt. The careful appliqué work and the precision of the quilting design make this quilt a classic, elegant piece.

NOTE

1. Barbara Brackman, *Clues in the Calico* (McLean VA: EPM Publications, Inc., 1989), 63.

QUILTMAKER:
Unknown

ORIGIN:
Location unknown, c. 1850–60

Cotton

QSPI 8

85" x 87"

1997.007.085

Plate 18

EAGLE APPLIQUÉ

The majestic eagle has symbolized strength and power for centuries. In 1782 the bald eagle, native only to North America, was declared our country's national bird and was incorporated in the great seal of the United States. The eagle then became a popular motif in eighteenth- and nineteenth-century decorative arts. The eagle is often portrayed, as in this quilt, with an olive leaf or branch in its beak.

The flowers that this quiltmaker chose to include in her quilt may reflect the appliquéd message of "Virtue, Liberty, and Independence, July Fourth 1776." The olive plant held by the eagle is a symbol of peace, as was first documented in ancient Greece. The tulip, draped within the swag border, may be a symbol of love. Lilies, pieced in a block format in the center of the quilt, are symbols of purity. Unfortunately we can't be sure of the quilter's intent. Though the quilt is inscribed "Dollie" on opposite corners, it entered the center's collection with no provenance.

Many eagle quilts made in the first half of the nineteenth century commemorate the signing of the Declaration of Independence. As the centennial of 1876 approached, eagles again became popular as a design motif. The later eagle quilts typically have four eagles, one in each corner, rather than the single-eagle format seen here.[1]

NOTE

1. Amelia Peck, *American Quilts & Coverlets in the Metropolitan Museum of Art* (New York: Metropolitan Museum of Art and Dutton Studio Books, 1990), 48.

QUILTMAKER:
Unknown

ORIGIN:
United States,
c. 1850–80

Cotton

QSPI 7

91" x 83"

1997.007.696

Plate 19
NORTH CAROLINA LILY

Rows of pieced lilies face one another on this quilt. A graceful appliquéd stem with a subtle curve and asymmetrically placed leaves counters the crisp line of the pattern. The lily is composed of two chevron shapes, in contrast to the more typical design that is constructed of four diamond shapes. The quiltmaker's difficulty in matching the two sides is evident in the extra fabric that is gathered to make the two pieces fit evenly together.

Different quilting designs highlight the bright lily pattern. The flowers are outlined with lines of stitches. In the large spaces between designs, a single plume drapes over a grid pattern. The stiff swag border, anchored by fabric bows, is softened with a quilted plume that emerges from its top and bottom.

Pieced floral designs are more unusual than appliquéd designs. The appliqué technique allows quilters to use realistically curved shapes in their patterns. Pieced floral designs produce more stylized versions of flowers.

QUILTMAKER:
Unknown

ORIGIN:
Probably United
States, c. 1850–70

Cotton

QSPI 11

88" x 88"

1997.007.307

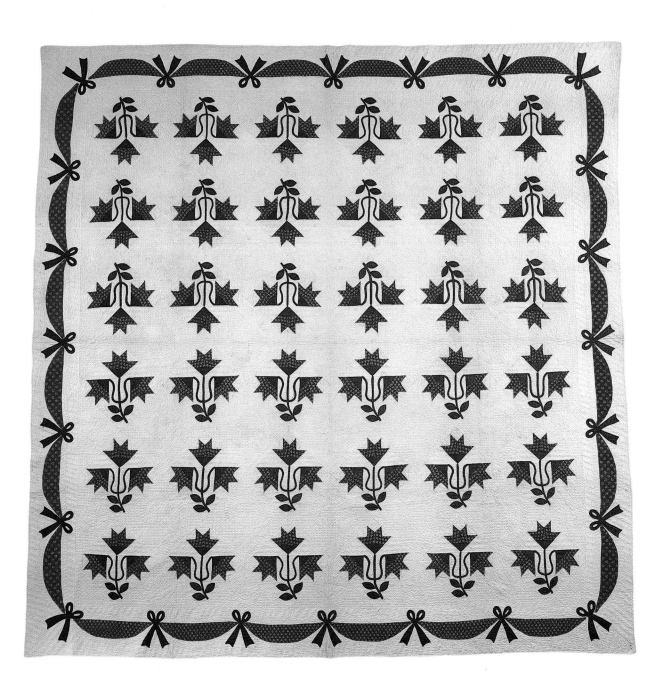

Plate 20

ROSE WREATH

A number of floral adaptations can be found in both the wreath design and border of this quilt. Simplified roses share a stem with what could be tulips or daffodils. The outer border alternates between a large cockscomb blossom and a trio of starflowers that share the same oversized leaf. An orange fabric, inset with a reverse appliqué technique for the cockscomb flower, adds a subtle contrast to the quilt's overall red-and-green palette.

Quilters in the mid–nineteenth century typically repeated a block pattern in the body of their quilts. For contrast they often added a unique border that incorporated original or unusual patterns, like the oversized leaf-and-plant combination used here. Many of the motifs found in the nineteenth-century appliqué quilts are similar to those found in other decorative arts of the period, such as painted tinware and furniture.

The rose wreath quilt is extravagantly quilted. In addition to echo quilting that follows the rose designs, the quilter stitched a number of unique elements. A plume is quilted along the edge of the oversized leaves in the border; and between the wreath appliqués we find similar quilted wreaths, rose designs, and a charming basket of flowers. Quilted leaves extend from the cockscomb blooms in the outer border, hearts are quilted in the tulip-shaped flowers from which tiny starflowers extend, and at the top of the quilt in the center, a pair of scissors lies ready.

QUILTMAKER:
Unknown

ORIGIN:
United States,
c. 1850–60

Cotton

QSPI 10

82″ x 84″

1997.007.275

Plate 21
COCKSCOMB

The tall leaf of the cockscomb plant contrasts with its beautiful fanlike flowers in this quilt. The distinctive plant was a popular choice for both American gardeners and quilters in the nineteenth century. In the years following the Civil War, gardeners ordered cockscomb seeds through mail-order catalogs. Tulips, also a perennial favorite, adorn the graceful curves of the quilt's outer border.

A tiny buttonhole stitch, using a single thread, outlines select areas of appliqué in this quilt. The stitch is used around the edges of the large tulips in the outer border and inside the square inset areas that lie between the green base and red petals of the cockscomb plants. The remaining appliquéd pieces are stitched with a simple whipstitch.

A sawtooth border frames the floral motifs. The triangles of the inner border culminate in a square at each corner. However, the maker needed a creative adjustment to make her outer triangular border fit the quilt. In the outside corners, the triangles have been "squeezed" together.

The red-and-green color combination of this quilt, set against a white background, creates a crisp, satisfying appearance. The background is filled with exquisitely quilted floral wreaths and feathers typical of mid-century quilts. The quilter also used a stipple quilting technique, in which background space is totally filled with stitches. The result is a richly textured surface that emphasizes the smooth designs of the appliquéd fabric pieces. The outer border is quilted in a carefully composed one-inch grid.

QUILTMAKER:
Unknown

ORIGIN:
Possibly Cumberland, Ohio, c. 1850–60

Cotton

QSPI 9

96" x 96"

1997.007.075

Plate 22
COCKSCOMB

The background of this quilt is unusual. Typically quiltmakers choose white backgrounds for their red-and-green appliqué quilts. The curious pink background fabric in this quilt is a chambray, or a fabric woven with colored warp yarns and white weft yarns. The underlying white yarns soften the effect of the pink color, yet it contrasts dramatically with the more typical colors of the four large blocks. The pink background suggests that this quilt may have been made by a quiltmaker of German descent. The quiltmaker probably lived in Pennsylvania, where a large number of German immigrants settled. This penchant for a colored background has been noted in other quilts of the period from southeastern Pennsylvania (northern Lancaster, Lebanon, and Berks Counties).[1]

The distinctive long leaf and fanlike bloom of the cockscomb plant were popular both in quilts and in gardens in the later years of the nineteenth century. The cockscomb, originally from tropical South America and Africa, is one of the few plants that was cultivated simply for its ornamental merit. Its value lies mostly in its flowers' longevity; the plush clusters of blossoms may last for as long as six to eight weeks.

The quiltmaker embroidered the following inscription on the corner of the quilt in white thread before the quilt was given to her granddaughter: "Quilt from Gram, age 65 years to Lattie Ben [Ban?] in 192[?]." We may estimate that "Gram" was born around 1855 and would have been in her twenties during the 1870s, a decade when the quiltmaker would have been a reasonable age for making this quilt and a period when this style quilt remained popular. Therefore we assign a probable date of 1870–80. However, without further research, we cannot be certain that the quilt was not made in the 1920s as is embroidered on the quilt.

While the appliquéd flowers are not as finely worked as many of the other floral designs featured in this catalog, carefully quilted feather wreaths provide a unifying element and demonstrate excellent quilting skills. The remaining background space is quilted with lines that run approximately one inch apart.

NOTE

1. Ricky Clark, *Quilted Gardens: Floral Quilts of the Nineteenth Century* (Nashville TN: Rutledge Hill, 1994), 21.

QUILTMAKER:
Unknown

ORIGIN:
Probably southeastern Pennsylvania, c. 1870–80

Cotton

QSPI 7

79.5″ x 77″

1997.007.123

Plate 23
WHIG ROSE VARIATION

The needlework in this Whig rose variation is exceptional: the appliqué motifs form diagonal lines across the quilt's plain background and frame richly quilted and stuffed floral sprays that include detailed roses and leaves. An unusual pink-striped fabric adds visual depth to the roses and buds, contrasting with the deep Turkey red calico fabric that accompanies it. The quiltmaker experienced difficulty in handling the vines in the borders. Only one corner flows easily; the others have simply run off the edge of the quilt or been joined clumsily. Also note the variations in the block pattern: the two and one half blocks in the bottom row are different from the others.

A quilted and stuffed strawberry motif is used alternately in the squares between the floral patterns. Stipple quilting also emphasizes the three-dimensional stuffed floral sprays. Echo quilting frames the large rose flowers central to the design.

QUILTMAKER:
Unknown

ORIGIN:
Possibly Ohio,
c. 1850–70

Cotton

QSPI 10

98" x 77"

1997.007.259

Plate 24
ROSE OF SHARON

This quilt's pattern is a variation of a very popular design known as the Whig rose. The pattern name rose of Sharon presumably alludes to the Song of Solomon found in the Bible's Old Testament. It is a poem about love and marriage in which the writer declares, "I am a rose of Sharon, a lily of the valley. As a lily among brambles, so is my love among maidens."[1]

Popular patterns like the rose of Sharon spread through society in a variety of ways during the nineteenth century. Agricultural fairs held in counties and states across the country were one of the major influences on pattern distribution.[2] The fairs, in which women participated as early as 1813, promoted the advancement of agriculture through education. Women were encouraged to enter their household goods in the "domestic or family manufacture" category, which encompassed foodstuffs such as bread, butter, and preserves and household textiles and quilts.

Subtle additions to the rose of Sharon pattern give this quilt a unique quality. For example, the centers of the flowers are embroidered. A single-thread yellow chain stitch spirals in a circle to create the flowers' pistils. A deliberately placed appliqué stitch is used on the plants' leaves and vines. Obviously different than the unseen stitch used on the red flowers, the appliqué stitch is sewn with a blue-green thread and is a regularly spaced whipstitch that extends slightly beyond the fabric's edge. The stitches emulate tiny barbs like those found on roses' leaves and stems. Four blue stems anchor the quilt's corners—perhaps the maker did not have enough green fabric to complete the quilt.

NOTES

1. Song of Sol. 2:1–2.
2. See Ricky Clark, *Quilted Gardens: Floral Quilts of the Nineteenth Century* (Nashville TN: Rutledge Hill, 1994), 85–91, and Virginia Gunn, "Quilts at Nineteenth-Century State and County Fairs: An Ohio Study," *Uncoverings* (1988): 108–28, for a discussion of the influence of agricultural fairs on quiltmaking.

QUILTMAKER:
Unknown

ORIGIN:
Possibly Pennsyl-
vania, c. 1850–70

Cotton

QSPI 9

85" x 84"

1997.007.539

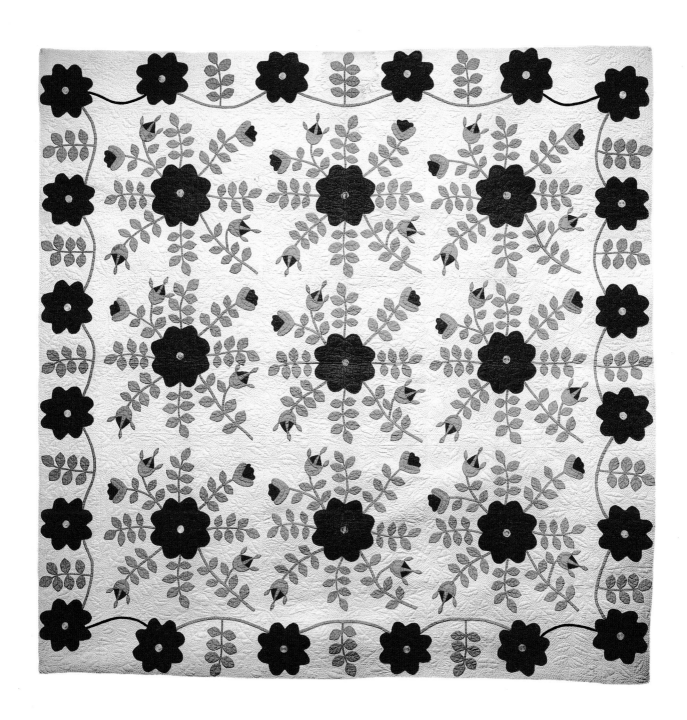

Plate 25
POTS OF FLOWERS

It is difficult to tell if this quilter had a particular plant in mind when she appliquéd her pattern or if she put the leaves of one plant together with the fruit of another simply to create a visually pleasing effect. The stylized balance of the pattern, incorporating a diamond shape for leaves and rigid lines as stems, contrasts with the flowing line of the outer border. The border is intricately interwoven, and its rounded shape is repeated in the clusters of berries that grow both on its vine and at the base of the potted plants. In the center of the quilt the maker quilted a Masonic symbol that incorporates a compass and a square. A feathered wreath is stitched in the areas between the plants, and a grid pattern fills the remaining space.

Quilters looked for inspiration for floral quilt motifs in their own gardens or in the flowers and leaves they gathered and pressed on nature outings. The flattened appearance of pressed plant specimens looks similar to the images we see in floral appliqué quilts. They could also find designs in the numerous garden magazines and catalogs that were published in the nineteenth century. Garden magazines carried simple line drawings that could easily be translated into appliqué patterns.

QUILTMAKER:
Unknown

ORIGIN:
Possibly Indiana,
c. 1850–70

Cotton

QSPI 9

80" x 86"

1997.007.870

Plate 26
POTS OF FLOWERS

Thistle-like plants balance in small vases in the four large blocks of this quilt. The flowers, or thistles, are made with a series of diamonds that the quiltmaker carefully stitched point to point, encircling the yellow centers. There are eighteen diamonds used in each flower—over two hundred in all.

The quilt's center wreath draws the pots of flowers together. Its shape is repeated in the feathered-wreath quilting pattern stitched in both the center of the appliquéd circle and in the large background areas that separate the pots of flowers. A slightly smaller version of the quilted wreath is sewn in the corners of the quilt.

In addition to the rhythmic feathered-wreath quilting, the maker added a double line of echo quilting that traces the shape of the plants. The remainder of the space within the border is filled with a diamond grid pattern. The large individual leaves tipped with red that slope in regular intervals around the quilt are surrounded by double lines of diagonal quilting. The leaves look like oversized budding Christmas cacti.

QUILTMAKER:
Unknown

ORIGIN:
Possibly Ohio,
c. 1850–70

Cotton

QSPI 9

81″ x 79″

1997.007.531

Plate 27
FLOWERS AND BUDS

The large, bright flowers of this design are constructed by layering a number of different fabrics on top of each other. The solid orange fabric in the center lies upon a green fabric with a tiny black print, which has been sewn over the solid red and solid green fabrics below. A small flower to the right of the layered blooms gives the pattern an asymmetrical balance. The oversized blossoms could represent a number of different flowers, such as dahlias or peonies, that American botanists had documented. Between the flowers, rings of berries are positioned around a green circle. Ten-point stars are quilted inside the ring.

North America was home to many unusual plants. One of the earliest botanists to study the wealth of plant life in the United States was John Bartram, regarded as the father of American botany. He settled on a farm near Philadelphia in 1728 and in thirty years of collecting sent specimens representing some two hundred North American species to England. The plants included the Virginia creeper, goldenrod, Michaelmas daisy, and staghorn sumac tree.

QUILTMAKER:
Unknown

ORIGIN:
Probably eastern or midwestern United States, c. 1860–80

Cotton

QSPI 9

77" x 76"

1997.007.898

Plate 28
POTS OF FLOWERS

The large, full blooms of this floral quilt may represent opulent Oriental poppies. They are surrounded by hundreds of small berries fabricated in both bright red and vivid green. Numerous stems, also laden with berries, extend horizontally from the center of each motif. The elements combine to create a bold appearance.

The quilt incorporates a four-block appliqué style that first appeared in American quilts in the mid–nineteenth century. However, the outer border—a smaller version of the potted plants—is very unusual. Red piping along the quilt's bound edge accentuates the vivid blossoms, and elaborate quilting echoes the floral motifs. Separate floral images are also quilted in the white background.

Poppies are one of a number of popular American plants first collected in the Orient. Although plants were collected in numerous countries, botanical studies in China were some of the most important due to the country's long history of skilled gardeners and its wealth of native plants. The Chinese didn't begin collecting and cataloging plants until the 1840s, at which time hundreds of species were introduced to the world. They included garden favorites like roses, lilies, primroses, rhododendrons, and azaleas.

QUILTMAKER:
Unknown

ORIGIN:
Possibly Ohio,
c. 1860–80

Cotton

QSPI 11

81.5" x 80.5"

1997.007.243

Plate 29
BASKETS OF FLOWERS

This bright quilt features a number of plants that are typically found at different times of the year—and all are growing on the same stem! A variety of tulips represent spring; large red and orange dahlias stand for summer; and oak leaves and jack-in-the-pulpit fruit symbolize fall.

A large dahlia-like flower dominates the composite plant growing in each of the four baskets. Imported from Mexico, dahlias were the most popular plants used for massing in flower beds in the nineteenth century. Late in the century, garden catalogs gave more space to dahlias than to any other flower. Today there are over two thousand varieties available.

Individual shapes are quilted throughout the white space of this quilt, placed without direction among the large floral motifs. Plumes, hearts, leaves, wreaths, flowers, and an unusual trefoil pattern are scattered throughout both the body of the quilt and the zig-zag border. The entire quilt is framed by a double binding that features an inner border of red piping and an outer border of green fabric.

QUILTMAKER:
Unknown

ORIGIN:
Possibly Pennsylvania or Ohio, c. 1860–80

Cotton

QSPI 8

87" x 80"

1997.007.013

Plate 30
FLORAL APPLIQUÉ

The bright red fabric used for the flowers in this quilt was a popular choice among quilters in the nineteenth century. It was called Turkey red because it was believed to have originated in the Turkish Ottoman Empire. In fact, the 1801 *Encyclopedia Britannica* entry referred to it as "that beautiful red dye which distinguishes the cottons manufactured in the Ottoman Empire." Today we know the process for producing the prized, colorfast, red cotton fabrics originated in India rather than in Turkey. By the mid–eighteenth century the dyeing process used for achieving the bright red cottons was being implemented in Europe, and the vivid fabrics, often featured in floral appliqué quilts, became more readily available.

The large-scale design of this quilt forms strong diagonal lines. In contrast, the vine that holds delicate grapes and flowers in the border sways gently. Quilting stitches soften the bold pattern of the floral design: between each motif the quilter stitched a gracefully curved plume. The border is quilted with a triple row of diagonal lines.

QUILTMAKER:
Unknown

ORIGIN:
Possibly Pennsyl-
vania, c. 1860–80

Cotton

QSPI 10

90.5" x 91.25"

1997.007.403

Plate 31

CALIFORNIA ROSE

Four large blocks, each centered with a two-color, circular rose and framed by four oak leaves, form the basic pattern of this quilt. Long, slender stems holding smaller roses create a secondary design in the blocks, which are surrounded by a jagged swag border. The swag is two layers of fabric carefully stitched down to maintain the numerous points this quiltmaker preferred. A grid pattern of quilting stitches covers the body of the quilt, while diagonal lines quilted in the border contrast with the drape of the appliquéd swags.

Roses have been a universal favorite for use in both gardens and quilts. Today there are more than one hundred known species of roses, with thirteen thousand varieties—all of which were propagated from fewer than ten species.

QUILTMAKER:
Unknown

ORIGIN:
Possibly Indiana,
c. 1860–80

Cotton

QSPI 12

90″ x 91″

1997.007.310

Plate 32
FLOWERS AND BUDS

Quilters did not always stitch flowers exactly as they saw them in their gardens. They sometimes used familiar shapes to make a pattern easier to sew. For example, in this quilt the maker used a star for the center of the flower and a diamond for the leaves on the outside border.

The overall design of this quilt is warm and inviting, with contrasting red and green colors, yet graceful and clean with its carefully planned pattern and extraordinary workmanship. The balance created by the quiltmaker is precise: the center of the floral motif is an eight-point star. The eight points are then repeated in the red petals of the flower and in the leaves and buds that protrude from the design's center. Sixteen blocks form the body of the quilt, which is then framed by a thin vine sprouting diamond-shaped leaves and a smaller version of the red flowers with star centers.

The floral designs in the central field are quilted using diagonal lines approximately one inch apart. The border is quilted with plumes that extend along both sides of the vine. Diagonal lines fill the remaining space in the border—these lines lie only about one-half inch apart. A feather shape is also used in the horizontal sashing between the floral blocks, while the vertical sashing is filled with an interlocking chain made with a double row of quilting stitches.

QUILTMAKER:
Unknown

ORIGIN:
Probably eastern
or midwestern
United States,
c. 1860–80

Cotton

QSPI 8

80" x 85"

1997.007.312

Plate 33

FLORAL APPLIQUÉ
WITH EAGLES

The eagle is often found in American quilts, expressing loyalty and patriotism, but it is unusual to find it used as the center of a flower. The contrast of bright red and golden orange fabrics is typical of quilts made in Pennsylvania and Ohio but is sometimes seen in quilts from other states as well.

Oriental poppies may have inspired the design of the flower used in this quilt. Particularly indicative of the poppy are the fernlike, deeply incised leaves of the plant and the rich red flowers in full bloom. The orange hue of the eagles may also be representative of the poppy, illustrating the golden yellow stamens of the flower. The Oriental poppy is native to the Middle East and Central Asia, as its name implies; however, there are twenty species of poppies native to western North America as well. The most popular is the California poppy.

Plumes are quilted in the outer border of the quilt, and echo quilting surrounds the unusual flowers. Faint pencil lines remain on the surface of the quilt—evidence of the manner in which the quilter marked her desired quilting pattern.

QUILTMAKER:
Unknown

ORIGIN:
Possibly Pennsyl-
vania, c. 1860–80

Cotton

QSPI 8

81″ x 79″

1997.007.144

Plate 34
MEXICAN ROSE

This rose pattern does not look like the roses seen on other quilts in this catalog. Each rose has six gently curved petals that make the flowers look as if they are swaying in the breeze. The fabric used for the petals of this stylized rose pattern features bright pink polka dots set on a red background. Orange centers are used in contrast to the polka-dot petals. A second, brighter, solid red fabric is used in the triangular sawtooth border.

A row of plumes is quilted between the solid red and sawtooth borders. Partial feather wreaths emerge from the inner border to form half circles that fill the triangular white spaces around the outside of the Mexican rose pattern. In the large diamond shapes between the floral motifs, the quilter added a variety of quilted floral bouquets that hold grapes, oak leaves, and flowers.

The pattern name may reflect the numerous plants from Mexico that were being imported into the United States during the period and becoming staples of the American garden. On the other hand, the quilt's pattern, a variation of the popular rose pattern, may indicate the maker's political awareness. Some believe the pattern got its name from a national issue being debated at mid-century: the Mexican War. The Mexican government did not accept Texas's independence and became embroiled in a one-sided war with the United States in 1846 when Texas was annexed as a state. The major political parties of the United States, the Whigs and the democrats, disagreed on the Union's involvement. They, too, lent their names to popular quilt patterns of the day (see cat. 14).

QUILTMAKER:
Unknown

ORIGIN:
Possibly Penn-
sylvania or Ohio,
c. 1860–80

Cotton

QSPI 9

99″ x 100.75″

1997.007.910

Plate 35
MEXICAN ROSE

The contrast of the deep red and brilliant yellow is dramatic in this quilt and may seem somewhat unusual. However, quilts with yellow or orange backgrounds instead of white grounds were popular in Pennsylvania in the last quarter of the nineteenth century. Some North Carolina quiltmakers of German descent also favored yellow backgrounds.[1] The rose pattern, frequently found in nineteenth-century appliqué quilts, has been simplified here and saved from a static appearance by the subtle bend of the roses' petals.

A detailed bouquet of flowers is quilted in the blocks of red fabric that alternate with the yellow squares. In the triangular red areas along the border of the quilt, a partial bouquet is quilted. Between the quilted designs the space is filled with a grid pattern. The flower petals and centers of the Mexican rose pattern and the red roses and buds of the border vine are stuffed to create a three-dimensional element.

NOTE

1. Ellen F. Eanes et al., *North Carolina Quilts* (Chapel Hill: University of North Carolina Press, 1988), 73, 92 (plates 3–9, 3–13, 3–25); Ricky Clark, *Quilted Gardens: Floral Quilts of the Nineteenth Century* (Nashville TN: Rutledge Hill, 1994), 21–23.

QUILTMAKER:
Unknown

ORIGIN:
Probably
Pennsylvania,
c. 1860–80

Cotton

QSPI 12

94″ x 92″

1997.007.877

Plate 36
FLORAL WREATH

The intertwined vines and flowers of this quilt create a dynamic pattern that seems to advance and recede as one looks at it. A wreath that holds a simple four-petal floral design alternates with a second wreath of roses. Orange tulip-like flowers sprout in opposite directions on all of the vines and accent the wreath motifs.

The interlocking pattern of the wreaths is similar to a gardening technique used for trees in some nineteenth-century gardens. Gardeners directed trees' growth so their branches intertwined to form screens, creating a style known as "pleached" trees. Open space between the trees was filled with a variety of box edgings or shrubs.

This quilt is hand pieced, but in contrast to most of the quilts in this catalog, it is machine quilted. Stitches follow the outer edge of the appliqué designs, and bountiful baskets of flowers and delicate floral sprays are quilted in the center of the floral wreaths. A double line quilted between the motifs sets the squares of the pattern apart.

QUILTMAKER:
Unknown

ORIGIN:
Probably eastern or midwestern United States, c. 1860–80

Cotton

Machine quilted

73" x 70"

1997.007.888

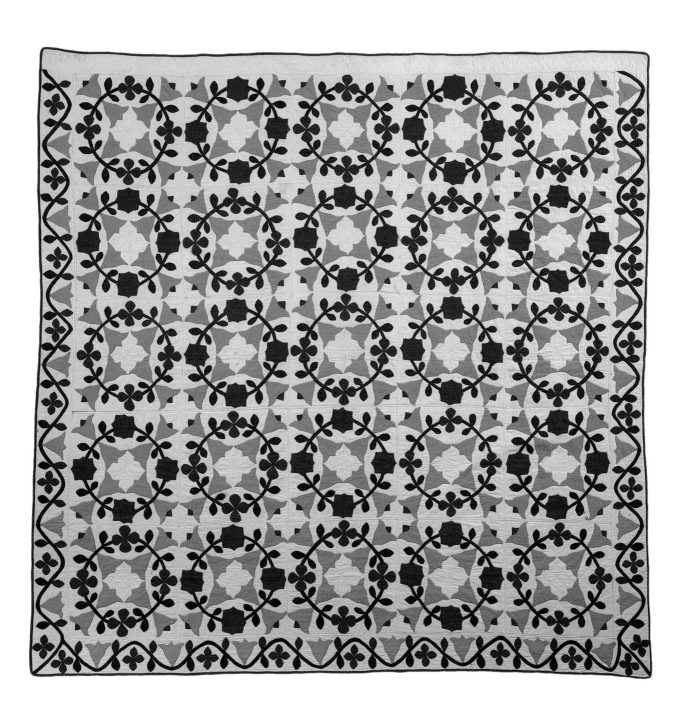

Plate 37

TEXAS STAR VARIATION
WITH TULIPS

While this quilt is similar in appearance to many others in the catalog, it is constructed very differently. The pattern is entirely pieced rather than appliquéd like the more typical floral designs. Piecing techniques, well suited for geometric patterns, are much more difficult when working with curved patterns. Rounded shapes require great skill: the quilter must ease the fabric around the shape and at the same time retain a flat surface. Appliqué gives quilters an opportunity to use a multitude of different shapes that are then stitched to the ground of the quilt.

Quilting stitches echo the shape of the tulip buds that extend from the center of each block, creating a sense of quivering motion. The space between the buds is quilted with double horizontal and vertical lines that form a straight grid.

Tulips, richly colored like those found in this quilt, were a particular favorite of gardeners past and present. In the sixteenth century, growers discovered that the plants, originally from Turkey, were well suited to the climate of the Netherlands. As a result, Dutch farmers began extensive tulip cultivation and hybridization. As unique variations of this species were introduced, public pressure for new bulbs increased until, in the seventeenth century, demand outgrew the supply. Prices rose dramatically—single bulbs could cost the equivalent of hundreds of dollars. The four-year craze (1634–37), called *Tulpenwoede* or "tulip mania," prompted Dutch businessmen to mortgage their homes and businesses in order to buy tulips to grow for the expanding market. In 1637, however, the market crashed, leaving many unfortunate speculators penniless.[1] In the nineteenth century, the presence of numerous tulip designs in chintz fabrics and stylized tulip patterns attest to the flower's continued popularity.

NOTE

1. Mike Dash, *Tulipomania: The Story of the World's Most Coveted Flower and the Extraordinary Passions It Aroused* (New York: Crown Publishing, 2000). For more about "tulip mania," see *La Tulipe noire* (1865) by Alexander Dumas, a French philosopher. Dumas's tale is one of love, jealousy, and greed, focusing on a prize offered for the hybridization of a new black tulip. It is available in the volume *The Black Tulip*, translated by A. J. O'Connor (New York: P. F. Collier and Son, 1902).

QUILTMAKER:
Unknown

ORIGIN:
Probably United
States, c. 1860–80

Cotton

QSPI 8

86.75" x 70.75"

1997.007.014

Plate 38

PINEAPPLE

The pineapple blocks of this quilt are complete with fruit and distinctive leaves. The large pineapple looks as though it is ripe, while the two smaller pineapples need more time on the vine. The format of the quilt, six blocks placed to face one another, is unusual. Typically we find either a four-block format or multiple-block designs of nine or more blocks.

The brown color of the pineapples, accompanied by dark green leaves, gives this appliqué quilt a subdued appearance that is contrasted by the exuberance of its design. The quilt-maker has pieced together small squares cut from a dark fabric to create the uneven gridlike pattern of the pineapple husk. The edges have been turned under and stitched down with a nearly invisible appliqué stitch. On two sides of the quilt, a simple trio of leaves sprout. Clamshell quilting is used throughout the quilt. Its radiating arcs soften the somewhat stiff appearance of the pineapples and the rigidity of the framed blocks.

The earliest written references to pineapples were by explorers Christopher Columbus and Gonzalo y Valdés, who noticed them growing in the West Indies. Pineapple was used there not only for food but also for winemaking. The Portuguese were largely responsible for disseminating the fruit, introducing it to both Africa and India in the 1500s. Before the end of that century, the cultivation of pineapples had spread to most of the tropical areas of the world.

QUILTMAKER:
Unknown

ORIGIN:
Possibly Kentucky,
c. 1860–80

Cotton

QSPI 9

90" x 79.5"

1997.007.282

Plate 39
BASKET

Pieced quilts with structurally identical blocks and no outer border, like this basket quilt, were popular in New England beginning about 1840. According to family tradition, this quilt descended from the Truman family of Rhode Island. Each block is set on point to accommodate the shape of the triangular basket and its delicate handle. Each basket holds a simple, stylized flower.

The quilting stitches form simple diagonal lines approximately one inch apart. The quilter used dark thread when quilting in the green fabric and white thread in the floral print used in the alternate blocks. The yellowish green color of the solid fabric appears to have been achieved by a dyeing process in which blue fabric was overdyed with yellow or vice versa. The blue dye, in this instance, was more fugitive, leaving behind green blocks with a yellowish cast.

Baskets are often featured in nineteenth-century quilts and may reflect a gardening trend that was popular in America during the 1830s and 1840s. Basket gardens were made by pushing either strips of wicker or wooden slats into the ground in a large oval shape. They were finished with a handle fastened over the top, and an assortment of brightly colored flowers were planted inside. Nineteenth-century gardening magazines frequently published descriptions of these flower beds and instructions for creating them.

QUILTMAKER:
Unknown

ORIGIN:
Probably
Providence,
Rhode Island,
c. 1860–80

Cotton

QSPI 7

90" x 89"

1997.007.694

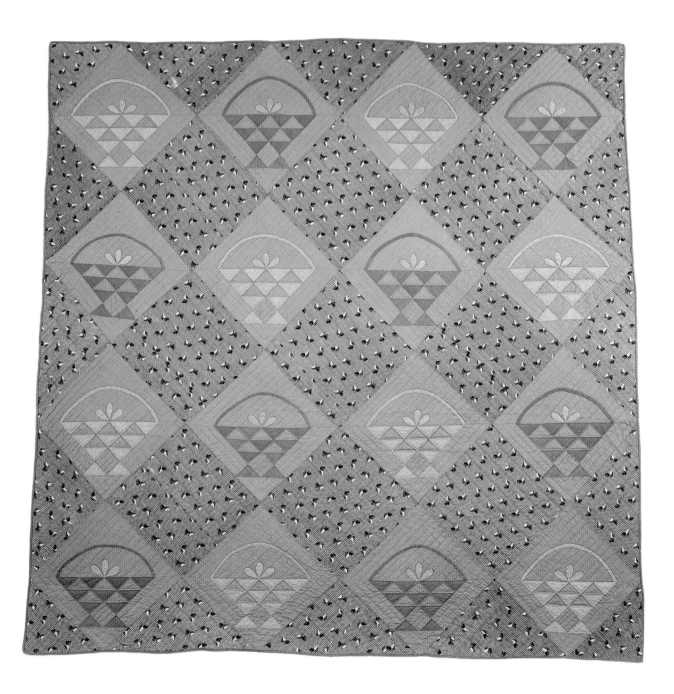

Plate 40
STARS AND LILIES

The lily pattern was a popular choice among quilters. The pattern traveled with settlers across the American continent, and different communities used different names for it. In the South the lily was typically called the North Carolina lily, in Ohio, the fire lily, and west of the Mississippi it was called a prairie lily. The lily pattern in this quilt is combined with an eight-point star. The pattern of the flower is actually half of the pieced star.

The maker of this quilt incorporated other sophisticated elements into her design.

For the stars and lilies she used an unusual green fabric printed with a bright pink nine-patch pattern. The fabric's nine-patch motif is repeated in the thin, green frames around the colorful stars and lilies; on a larger scale, it is used in the body of the quilt, where the nine patch is formed by alternating framed-star and lily blocks. Four lily blocks with floral printed backgrounds accent the motif.

In the outer border of this quilt, a four-band cable quilting pattern still retains dark pencil lines that were drawn on to mark the lines for quilting. In addition to the cable quilting in the border, the quilter covered the entire center of the quilt with a diagonal grid.

QUILTMAKER:
Unknown

ORIGIN:
Possibly Pennsylvania, c. 1860–80

Cotton

QSPI 6

84" x 84"

1997.007.216

Plate 41
PINE TREE

Except for the trunk of the pine tree pattern, all of the pieces of this quilt use the same triangular shape. Even the border, a variation of the flying geese pattern, uses a series of triangles in its design. They are placed and stitched together with great precision, each point clearly defined.

The entire surface of this quilt is covered with quilting. Feather wreaths are quilted in the large open spaces between the pine trees and in the space between the motifs and the border. The spaces inside the quilted wreaths and in the open areas between the motifs are filled with a grid pattern. The outer border repeats the linear theme, quilted with a single diagonal line.

The white pine tree of North America was an important resource for shipbuilding. A full-grown pine could grow to reach up to eighty feet, making it ideal for the masts of the great sailing ships of the seventeenth and eighteenth centuries. In fact, in the mid-1700s England adopted the "broad arrow" policy, giving it the right to take for commercial use any white pines with at least a twenty-four-inch diameter found along the northeast coast of what would become the United States. The trees to be cut down were marked with an arrow, hence the term "broad arrow."

According to family records, this quilt was made by the grandmother of a Mrs. Hutchins of Indiana, Pennsylvania. The quilt was given to Mrs. Hutchins when she was seven years old, upon the death of her mother.

QUILTMAKER:
Grandmother of
Mrs. Hutchins

ORIGIN:
Indiana, Pennsyl-
vania, c. 1860–80

Cotton

QSPI 9

69" x 69"

1997.007.408

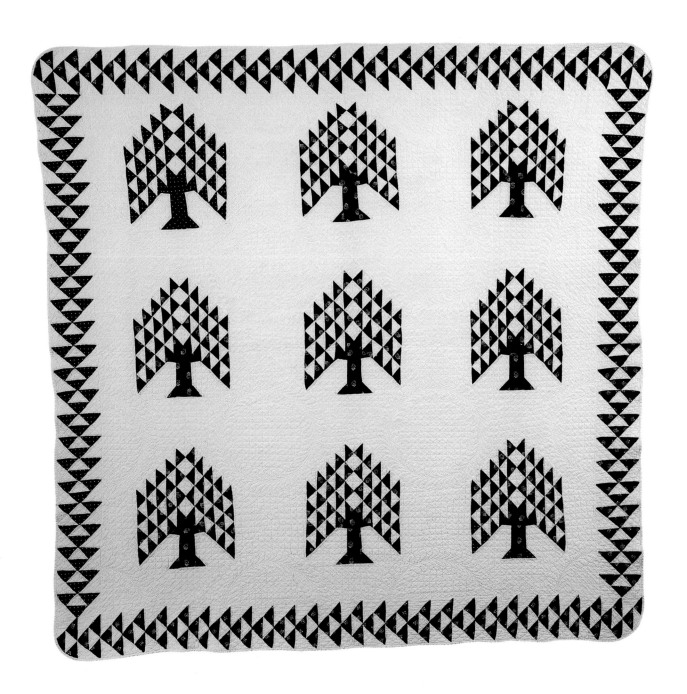

Plate 42
SUNNYSIDE ALBUM

Students from the Sunnyside Academy gave this album quilt, with a series of different block designs, to their teacher Eli Hoke. It is proudly embroidered: "Presented by your scholars at Sunnyside, Ohio, 1874." In another block his students requested: "Accept our valued friendship and roll it up[?] in cotton, and think it not illusion because so easily gotten." Both Hoke's name and the students' names are embroidered on the quilt among an abundance of baskets, floral wreaths, and flowers (see chart).

The appearance of the quilt has changed since its origin. Many of the fabrics that today appear tan were originally green. The dye or combination of dyes used to produce the green fabrics were fugitive, and, thus, all of the once-green fabric has faded to a disappointing tan.

A great variety of skill levels are evident in the appliqué and pieced designs of this album quilt. The quilt also includes numerous stitching techniques. For example, the pieced patterns are both hand and machine stitched. The quilting stitches, however, are very consistent and seem to be the work of one individual. The quilting stitches form a variety of designs: interlocking rings, flowers, plumes, crosses, hearts, and a pair of eyeglasses. Perhaps Mr. Hoke wore glasses.

Accept our valued friendship,
And roll it up in cotton,
And think it not illusion,
Because so easily gotten.

ELI

Hoke.

Johnnie Markley.

Callie   Christy

Amos

Emma Fasick

INSCRIPTIONS:

1. W. Hisson[s] 8

2. Warren Fasick

3. Mamie Critton

4. Maggie Fasick

5. Nora Johnston

6. Pearly Harshbarger

7. Anson Hill

8. Phillip Christy

9. Joseph W.

10. Eva Critton

11. E+ L+ M+

12. Clara H.

13. Johnnie Ditmer

14. Luie Critton

15. Ira Shatzley

16. Orin Ditmer

17. Ira Wright

18. Loa Ruterbaugh

19. In God We Trust

20. Albert Critton

21. MJ

22. With respect, Ethel

23. Dora Cassell

24. Roy Hisson[s]

25. Presented by your scholars at Sunnyside, Ohio 1874

26. Ada Miller

27. Minnie Christy

28. Bertha Markley

29. Accept our valued friendship / and roll it up[?] in cotton / and think it not illusion / because so easily gotten.

30. Eli Hoke

31. Dora Christy

32. Willie Critton

33. John Ruterbaugh

34. Wright

35. Johnnie Markley

36. Callie Christy

37. Cora and Luie Ditmer

38. Amos Hill

39. Emma Fasick

40. Rosa H.

41. Oscar W.

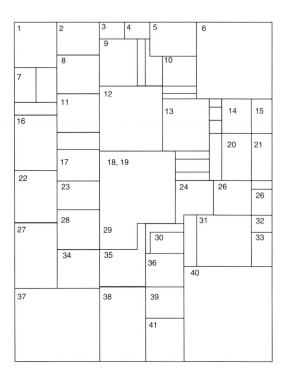

QUILTMAKER:
Includes various signatures

ORIGIN:
Darke County, Ohio, dated 1874

Cotton

QSPI 11–12

90" x 66"

1997.007.916

Plate 43
FLOWER GARDEN MOSAIC

This quilter carefully chose fabrics to create a pattern of concentric hexagons that resembles rows of flowers growing in a structured flower bed. Together the hexagons form rows of alternating color. Those set on a background of light orange fabric with black polka dots form a large hexagon themselves. The outer border of flowers framed with bright red, square blocks forms a fence around the ordered rows of the flourishing garden.

Hexagons are first found in American quilts of the early nineteenth century and are believed to be a result of the transmission of English paper-piecing techniques to America.[1] In this technique, fabric is first gathered around a paper template. Each hexagon is then carefully sewn together to form a larger pattern.

Hexagons became popular again in the latter years of the nineteenth century. Amelia Peck, author of *American Quilts & Coverlets*, explains that the popularity of hexagon quilts in the 1870s and 1880s was a response to the Moorish, or Turkish, style of home decorating that became fashionable at that time.[2] Magazines recommended hexagon quilts as an appropriate addition to exotically decorated rooms. The decorating style is an example of the enormous interest in Eastern cultures that swept Europe and the Americas in the nineteenth century.

NOTES

1. Virginia Gunn, "Victorian Silk Template Patchwork in American Periodicals, 1850–1875," *Uncoverings* (1983): 9–28.
2. Amelia Peck, *American Quilts & Coverlets in the Metropolitan Museum of Art* (New York: Metropolitan Museum of Art and Dutton Studio Books, 1990), 73.

QUILTMAKER:
Unknown

ORIGIN:
Possibly New England, c. 1870–90

Cotton

QSPI 7

80" x 86"

1997.007.238

Plate 44
PINE TREE

The simple repetition of this pine tree pattern, composed primarily of triangles, contrasts with the graceful plumes that are quilted in the outer border. The triangular pattern is repeated in a simple but effective dark border that frames the trees.

The diagonal grid of the quilting pattern in this quilt is typical of nineteenth-century quilts; however, this quilter stitched over both the pine trees and the background alike. As in several other quilts in this catalog, pencil lines drawn in to guide the quilter's needle remain visible.

In Chinese and Japanese cultures, pine trees often symbolize strength and longevity, due to the fact that they remain green all winter, withstanding extreme weather conditions, and because they may live for centuries. In America, pine trees are often identified with the landscape of northern New England. During the Revolution, the first floating batteries on the Charles River flew flags that displayed a pine tree. Today, Maine's flag retains the pine tree symbol.

QUILTMAKER:
Unknown

ORIGIN:
Possibly Ohio,
c. 1870–90

Cotton

QSPI 9

83" x 82"

1997.007.130

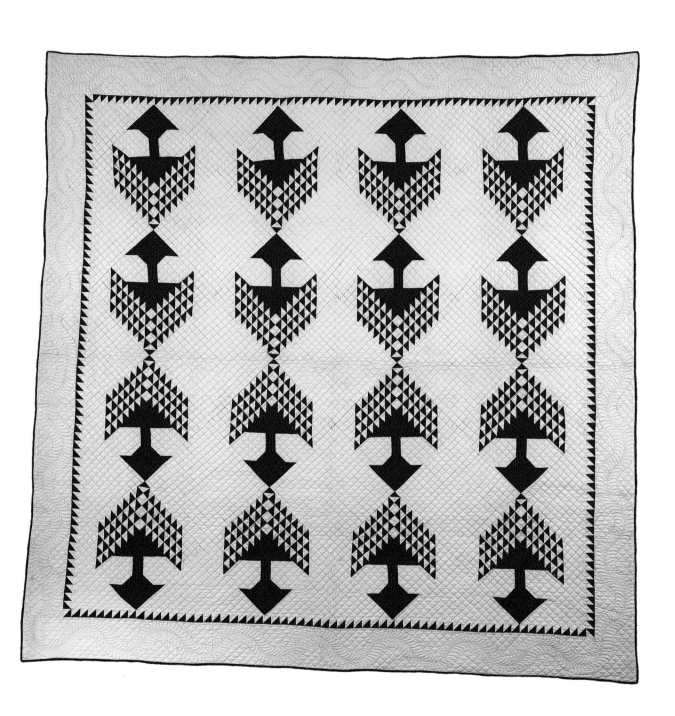

Plate 45
CAROLINA LILY

A vivid pink stripe running through a strip of
bright green fabric separates the triangular
shape of the Carolina lily motifs in this quilt. A
large variety of fabrics, including prints, plaids,
and checks, make up the lilies, creating a riot
of color that is contained by the strong lines of
the diagonal sashing. The lily motifs are hand
sewn, but the long seams found in the sashing
are machine stitched.

Today, a number of plants that are not related
to the lily family share this common, vernac-
ular name. True lilies are tall, erect plants
with narrow leaves and flowers that comprise
six petal-like segments that form the shape
of a trumpet. This quilt pattern, although
stylized, does offer a realistic image of the
true lily.

QUILTMAKER:
Unknown

ORIGIN:
Probably United
States, c. 1880–
1900

Cotton

QSPI 7

84" x 80"

1997.007.042

Plate 46
FLORAL WREATH

Paulina Herdrich signed and dated her quilt 1890 in red chain-stitch embroidery. She chose an appliqué pattern with a series of repeated blocks that looks similar to many of the other red-and-green appliqué quilts in this catalog. Paulina, however, created a unique border that includes birds, insects, and animals marching around the four edges. She included a peacock, dragonfly, elephant, and giraffe in her quilt border, with charming disregard for scale. She also included an anchor, hatchet, boot, and pipe. Perhaps the figures were from the family farm—but no typical farm in America housed a bear (or wolf) that walked with a cane or a resident alligator! Paulina also used embroidery to add details to the animals found in her intriguing border.

The roses of the central wreaths are a single piece of fabric whose petals are detailed by quilting stitches. The leaves of the wreaths hold quilted hearts, and echo quilting outlines many of the appliquéd shapes. Wreaths are a common design element in many quilt appliqué patterns and in the decorative arts in general. They also have a long history of use in religious rituals. For example, during the fifteenth and sixteenth centuries, wreaths, especially ones made of roses, were worn as adornment in weddings, festivals, and pageants. In the nineteenth century, carved wooden wreaths became popular architectural elements.

QUILTMAKER:
Paulina Herdrich

ORIGIN:
Marion County,
Ohio, dated 1890

Cotton

QSPI 8

87" x 69"

1997.007.878

Plate 47
OAK REEL

Borders of appliqué quilts were a favorite place for quiltmakers to demonstrate their creativity. Caroline Ruth, the maker of this quilt according to family information, incorporated into her border various amusing images. Scattered among the assorted wild and domesticated animals, one can find a man, his pipe and boots, an axe, a hammer, and other tools. Caroline also added urns, baskets, and pots to her image-filled border. The satisfied cat and the lovebirds are emblems of domestic tranquility and happiness.

Caroline Ruth was born in 1838 and died in 1907, at nearly seventy years of age. She married a farmer, Charles Ruth, and raised seven children. Her obituary read: "Nearly her whole life was spent in Richland township. She was a Christian woman with a host of friends."[1]

A second quilt from the James Collection is very similar to Caroline's. The quilt pictured in plate 46, a floral wreath pattern made by Paulina Herdrich in 1890 in Marion County, Ohio, contains a series of appliqué blocks framed by a border that contains nearly all of the same figures found in Paulina's. It appears that the two women may have worked together on their quilts, but no documentation is available to support this hypothesis.

NOTE

1. Genealogical research was done by Stacy Epstein, former curator of the Ardis and Robert James Collection.

QUILTMAKER:
Caroline Ruth

ORIGIN:
Marion County,
Ohio, dated 1889

Cotton

92" x 67.5"

1997.007.429

Plate 48

ROSEBUD

The repeated rosebud blocks of this quilt are framed with green sashing that is beginning to show signs of fading. The large red flowers are offset by yellow centers that are blanket stitched in place. Around the outer edge of the quilt, the maker added a floral chintz border that retains the bright blue of its blue-and-buff color combination. The buff is most likely the remains of a pink or lavender dye that lost its color due to light exposure or washing.

The appliqué technique used to create the large-scale rose pattern is unusual. The fabric edges have been turned under, but rather than first stitching them down, it appears the maker has used quilting stitches to secure the design elements in place. These stitches were sewn in brown thread, while the remaining quilting stitches were done in a more conventional white thread. The long leaves that enclose the red buds are stuffed with extra batting.

Roses, a popular flower among American quilters, have been used as a decorative motif for centuries. They were brought to France and England from Asia in the Middle Ages and became symbolic in various ways throughout Western society. In fifteenth-century England, a red or a white rose represented the families fighting for the English Crown in what became known as the War of the Roses. Early Christians used the rose as a symbol of faith. Eighteenth-century poets and painters proclaimed the rose as a symbol of romance and beauty. It became a popular design in wallpaper and fabrics of the nineteenth century.

QUILTMAKER:
Unknown

ORIGIN:
Possibly Pennsyl-
vania, c. 1890–
1920

Cotton

QSPI 8

96″ x 88″

1997.007.667

Plate 49
CRAZY QUILT

A number of typical motifs found in crazy quilts are illustrated in this quilt. Fans, flowers, and butterflies can be found arranged around a center block that features a horseshoe draped in berries and framing a sunflower. Horseshoes are known as a symbol of good luck, and sunflowers were described as symbols of adoration in many of the nineteenth-century books on the language of flowers.

The increased availability of silk by the end of the nineteenth century made it affordable for middle-class women to create luxurious silk quilts for display. These fancy quilts were not meant for use as bedcovers; women instead draped them over a sofa or table as a way of showing off their superior needle skills. Crazy quilts were most popular between 1880 and 1910.

Most crazy quilts do not have quilting stitches holding their different layers together. Instead, the top is constructed by sewing the various unusually shaped pieces to a foundation fabric. A cloth back is then added. The three layers may be tied together with thread or embroidery floss to hold them in place, though this quiltmaker has not used either of those methods. On this crazy, the backing is simply hemmed to the top with a whipstitch around the edge of the quilt. A decorative scalloped lace trim frames the quilt.

QUILTMAKER:
Unknown

ORIGIN:
Possibly Ohio,
c. 1875–90

Silk

No quilting

64″ x 68″

1997.007.670

Plate 50
CRAZY QUILT

Lizzie M. Bradley made this crazy quilt in 1884: she proudly embroidered her name and the date at the top of the quilt. In the center block she embroidered an elaborate monogram with a date of 1883. Perhaps the dates refer to the beginning and end of Lizzie's work on the quilt. Lizzie also included a number of embroidered elements that are typically found in crazy quilts: a peacock, fans, flowers, and butterflies. For an unusual touch, she used hexagons to create simple flowers in various areas of the quilt.

A technique called ribbon embroidery was used to create many of the flowers of this crazy quilt. The technique involves gathering and folding ribbons into the shape of a desired flower and then stitching them into place. Lizzie created numerous roses, daisies, zinnias, and lilacs with ribbon embroidery, giving her quilt a three-dimensional quality. Lizzie also used an interesting embroidery stitch to outline the square blocks of her crazy quilt. It is an eight-point star pattern with a French knot at the end of each point. Hundreds of French knots adorn the quilt's surface!

QUILTMAKER:
Lizzie M. Bradley

ORIGIN:
Probably United
States, dated
1883–84

Silk, velvet

No quilting

67" x 67"

1997.007.803

Plate 51
CRAZY QUILT
WITH SCRIPTURE

This quilt was made for Frances Willard by her mother, Mary T. Willard. Because the year cross-stitched on the quilt corresponds with the year of Frances's fiftieth birthday (28 September 1889), the quilt presumably was a fiftieth birthday present. Frances Willard was a pivotal figure in the United States suffrage and temperance movements. In 1874 she became the national president of the Women's Christian Temperance Union, the largest women's organization in the United States. She led the WCTU in its campaign for social reforms such as prohibition, women's right to vote, and home protection.

Many of the fabrics included on the quilt have floral designs and scriptural quotes embroidered on them. Flowers had a symbolic language that many nineteenth-century people could read, thus the message of this quilt is reflected not only in the Biblical verse but also in the floral designs it incorporates. The daisies may represent innocence; the lilacs, humility; and the violets, fidelity.

Mrs. Willard cross-stitched the scriptural phrases with various thick wool yarns. Many of her floral designs are embroidered with a satin stitch, which completely fills the pattern's space with an even stitch. She also used a Kensington stitch, which similarly fills an entire space but does so with a series of stitches in various lengths. The Kensington stitch gives more of a painterly effect.[1] Mrs. Willard chose to use typical crazy-quilt stitches along the quilt's seams, including the herringbone, buttonhole, and coral stitches, but many of her embroidered patterns are composite stitches. For example, a zigzag buttonhole stitch with a straight stitch and French knots was commonly used.

In the 1880s, nearly all of the leading women's magazines included printed patterns for embroidery. In addition to being used on crazy quilts, these patterns were suggested for use on towels, tablecloths, scarves, and handkerchiefs.[2]

NOTES

1. Penny McMorris, *Crazy Quilts* (New York: E. P. Dutton, 1984), 20.
2. McMorris, *Crazy Quilts,* 31.

EMBROIDERED VERSES:

1. The Steps of a good man are ordered by the Lord.

2. God is love.

3. Many are the afflictions of the righteous, but the Lord delivereth him out of them all.

4. Delight thyself also in the Lord, and he shall give thee the desires of thy heart.

5. Be not overcome of evil but overcome evil with good.

6. Lo, I am with you alway[s] even unto the end of the world.

7. The just shall live by faith.

8. Beloved now are we the sons of God and it doth not yet appear what we shall be, but we know that when he shall appear we shall be like him, for we shall see him as he is.

9. Let us not weary in well doing, for in due season we shall reap if we faint not.

10. We know that we passed from death unto life because we love the brethren.

11. In all the ways acknowledge him, and he shall direct thy paths.

12. To be carnally minded is death, but to be spiritually minded is life and peace.

13. Look unto me and be ye saved.

14. Come unto me all ye that labor and are heavy laden, and I will give you rest. Take my yoke upon you and learn of me, for I am meek and lowly in heart, and ye shall find rest to your souls. For my yoke is easy and my burden is light.

15. A soft answer turneth away wrath.

16. Trust we in the Lord forever for in the Lord Jehovah is everlasting strength.

17. Made for Frances Willard by her mother Mary T. Willard. Dec.

18. A merry heart is a continual feast.

19. The lord is nigh unto them that call upon him, to all that call upon him in truth.

20. There remaineth therefore a rest to the people of God.

21. The effectual fervent prayer of a righteous man availeth much.

22. The Angel of the Lord encampeth roud [round] about them that fear him and delivereth him.

23. By humility and fear of the Lord are riches, honor, and life.

24. I shall be satisfied when I wake with thy likeness.

25. Jesus wept.

26. And they shall be mine sayeth the Lord of hosts in that day when I make up my jewels and I will spare them as a man spareth his own son the seeveth[?] him.

27. If ye love me, keep my commandments.

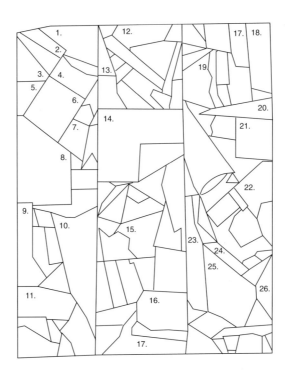

QUILTMAKER:
Mary T. Willard

ORIGIN:
Evanston, Illinois, dated 1889

Wool

No quilting

85" x 67"

1997.007.318

Plate 52
CRAZY QUILT

In the lower left block of this sumptuous crazy quilt, a majestic eagle carries an American flag and holds a banner reading "E Pluribus Unum," translated as "out of many, one." The notation "14th A.C." in the same block may refer to a military company.

Many three-dimensional flowers are featured on the blocks of this crazy quilt. In the center, against a blue velvet fabric, carefully layered pink roses glimmer alongside an elaborately embroidered monogram. Above the roses, red cockscomb blossoms take hold next to fuschia flowers and apple blossoms. Below the center block, a stalk of goldenrod, stitched with thick yarns that create a textured effect, is framed by Queen Anne's lace. Butterflies float among daisies, lilacs, and tulips. The numerous floral designs are reflected in the elaborate embroidery stitches that embellish the seams of the crazy quilt's blocks: small flowers are highlighted with French knots; long grasses support tiny buds.

Tall, stiff-stemmed flowers were in fashion in the 1880s—daisies, goldenrod, cockscomb, and lilies, for example. Their popularity may be due to an exhibit at the Philadelphia Centennial Exposition in 1876, where England's Royal School of Art Needlework embroideries were displayed. The embroideries featured these types of plants.

QUILTMAKER:
Unknown

ORIGIN:
Possibly Indiana,
c. 1880–1900

Silk

No quilting

70" x 70"

1997.007.284

Plate 53
FLORAL ALBUM

The symbolic messages of the floral imagery in this quilt may indicate that it is a memorial quilt. The cross amidst a spray of flowers (second row from top, second block from left) and the black silk fabric used for the background, an unusual choice, also support this theory. The quiltmaker likely considered the language of flowers that was popular in the nineteenth century when sewing this quilt. The primroses may symbolize childhood, the poppies, time and its passage. Anemones often symbolized forsakenness or the winter of life.

The quilter used a whipstitch to attach the numerous fabric pieces to her quilt. Layered fabrics and embroidered details add to the realism of the floral bouquets. Thread is coiled around itself to create centers for some flowers; other flowers have embroidered stars for centers. Extra stuffing gives some flowers a three-dimensional quality, while others have embroidered outlines stitched in contrasting colors. Tiny white stitches on the surface of the red strawberries emulate seeds found on the outer surface of the fruit.

In contrast to the fanciful flowers found on most of the quilts in this catalog, this quilt features an impressive collection of realistic flowers. Many of them appear as simple clusters that look as if they were just picked, but others are carefully tied with delicate bows. Near the center of the quilt, one floral group is planted in what may be a basket garden—a woven planter of wicker or wooden slats.

QUILTMAKER:
Unknown

ORIGIN:
Possibly Philadelphia, Pennsylvania, c. 1910–20

Cotton, wool, silk

QSPI 5–6

87" x 86"

1997.007.125

SELECTED BIBLIOGRAPHY

BOTANY AND GARDENING REFERENCES

Abir-Am, Pnina, and Dorinda Outram, eds. *Uneasy Careers and Intimate Lives: Women in Science, 1789–1979.* New Brunswick NJ: Rutgers University Press, 1987.

Adams, William H. *Nature Perfected: Gardens through History.* New York: Abbeville, 1991.

Alic, Margaret. *Hypatia's Heritage.* Boston: Beacon, 1986.

Arnold, Lois B. *Four Lives in Science: Women's Education in the Nineteenth Century.* New York: Schocken Books, 1984.

Benjamin, Marina, ed. *Science & Sensibility: Gender and Scientific Inquiry, 1780–1945.* Oxford: Basil Blackwell, 1991.

Breck, Joseph. *New Book of Flowers.* New York: O. Judd, Co., 1866.

Dash, Mike. *Tulipomania: The Story of the World's Most Coveted Flower and the Extraordinary Passions It Aroused.* New York: Crown Publishing, 2000.

Downing, Andrew J. *Cottage Residences.* New York: Wiley & Putnam, 1842.

Dumas, Alexandre. *The Black Tulip.* Trans. A. J. O'Connor. New York: P. F. Collier and Son, 1902.

Ehrenreich, Barbara, and Deirdre English. *Witches, Midwives, and Nurses: A History of Women Healers.* Old Westbury NY: Feminist Press, 1973.

Gates, Barbara T., and Ann B. Shteir, eds. *Natural Eloquence: Women Reinscribe Science.* Madison: University of Wisconsin Press, 1997.

Heiser, Charles B., Jr. *Seed to Civilization.* Cambridge: Harvard University Press, 1990.

Henderson, Peter. *Gardening for Pleasure.* New York: Orange Judd Co., 1887.

Kremers, Edward, and George Urdang. *History of Pharmacy.* Philadelphia: J. B. Lippencott Company, 1940.

Leighton, Ann. *American Gardens of the Nineteenth Century.* Amherst: University of Massachusetts Press, 1987.

Lewis, Walter H., and Memory P. F. Elvin-Lewis. *Medical Botany.* New York: John Wiley & Sons, 1977.

Morton, A. G. *History of Botanical Science.* London: Academic Press, 1981.

Phillips, Patricia. *The Scientific Lady: A Social History of Women's Scientific Interests, 1520–1918.* London: Weidenfeld and Nicolson, 1990.

Rossiter, Margaret W. *Women Scientists in America: Struggles and Strategies to 1940.* Baltimore: Johns Hopkins University Press, 1982.

Shteir, Ann B. *Cultivating Women, Cultivating Science: Flora's Daughters and Botany in England, 1760 to 1860.* Baltimore: Johns Hopkins University Press, 1996.

Tippo, Oswald, and William L. Stern. *Humanistic Botany.* New York: W. W. Norton & Company, 1977.

Visher, Stephen S. *Scientists Starred, 1903–1943,*

in *"American Men of Science."* Baltimore: Johns Hopkins University Press, 1947.

Wharton, Edith. *Italian Villas and Their Gardens.* New York: Century Co., 1904.

TEXTILE AND QUILT HISTORY REFERENCES

Adamson, Jeremy. *Calico and Chintz: Antique Quilts from the Collection of Patricia S. Smith.* Washington DC: Smithsonian Institution, Renwick Gallery, 1997.

Atkins, Jacqueline, and Phyllis Tepper. *New York Beauties: Quilts from the Empire State.* New York: Dutton Studio Books, 1992.

Brackman, Barbara. *Clues in the Calico.* McLean VA: EPM Publications, Inc., 1989.

Clark, Ricky. *Quilted Gardens: Floral Quilts of the Nineteenth Century.* Nashville TN: Rutledge Hill, 1994.

Clark, Ricky, ed. *Quilts in Community: Ohio's Traditions.* Nashville TN: Rutledge Hill, 1991.

Crews, Patricia Cox and Ronald C. Naugle, eds. *Nebraska Quilts & Quiltmakers.* Lincoln: University of Nebraska Press, 1991.

Eanes, Ellen Fickling, Erma Hughes Kirkpatrick, Sue Barker McCarter, Joyce Joines Newman, Ruth Haislip Roberson, and Kathlyn Fender Sullivan. *North Carolina Quilts.* Ed. Ruth Haislip Roberson. Chapel Hill: University of North Carolina Press, 1988.

Goldsborough, Jennifer. *Lavish Legacies: Baltimore Albums and Related Quilts in the Collection of the Maryland Historical Society.* Baltimore: Maryland Historical Society, 1994.

McMorris, Penny. *Crazy Quilts.* New York: E. P. Dutton, 1984.

Peck, Amelia. *American Quilts & Coverlets in the Metropolitan Museum of Art.* New York: Metropolitan Museum of Art and Dutton Studio Books, 1990.

GENERAL DESIGN REFERENCES

Gere, Charlotte, and Michael Whiteway. *Nineteenth-Century Design: From Pugin to Mackintosh.* New York: Harry N. Abrams, 1994.

Kaplan, Wendy. *"The Art That Is Life": The Arts and Crafts Movement in America, 1875–1920.* Boston: Little, Brown and Company, 1987.

Motz, Marilyn Ferris, and Pat Browne, eds. *Making the American Home: Middle-Class Women and Domestic Material Culture, 1840–1940.* Bowling Green OH: Bowling Green State University Popular Press, 1988.

THE CONTRIBUTORS

Margaret R. Bolick is curator of the Division of Botany of the University of Nebraska State Museum. She received her undergraduate and master's degrees from Duke University and her Ph.D. from the University of Texas at Austin. She is a co-instructor for the course History and Philosophy of Museums in the museum studies program. Her research interests include pathology, the study of pollen, and the history of women in botany. She continues to gather information on female students at the University of Nebraska during the period 1876–1915 and would like to hear from readers who have information about any of these women.

Patricia Cox Crews is a professor of textiles and the director of the International Quilt Study Center at the University of Nebraska–Lincoln. Crews was born and raised in a small town in the Shenandoah Valley of Virginia but has lived in the Midwest—Kansas and Nebraska—for more than twenty years. She earned her bachelor's degree from Virginia Tech, where she majored in fashion design. She has a master's degree in textile science from Florida State University, and she completed her Ph.D. at Kansas State University, where her specialization was in textiles, with a minor in American history. Crews has published more than fifty technical papers about the history, conservation, and performance properties of textiles. *Nebraska Quilts and Quiltmakers* (Lincoln: University of Nebraska Press, 1991), for which she served as primary editor and author of

several chapters, won the Smithsonian's Frost Prize for Distinguished Scholarship in American Crafts in 1993.

Susan Curtis grew up in Iowa and learned quilting and sewing from her grandmothers. She received her master's degree in museum studies from the University of Nebraska. Her experience with textile collections includes work with the International Quilt Study Center, the ethnographic textiles in the Division of Anthropology of the University of Nebraska State Museum, the National Museum of Roller Skating, and the historical textiles in the Department of Textiles, Clothing, and Design at the University of Nebraska. She is an enthusiastic textile historian and gardener and served as a curatorial assistant for the exhibit *Fanciful Flowers: Botany and the American Quilt.*

Carolyn Ducey is the curator of the James Quilt Collection at the International Quilt Study Center at the University of Nebraska–Lincoln. She is a native Nebraskan, born and raised in Omaha. She received her bachelor's degree in art history from the University of Nebraska at Omaha and then attended Indiana University, where she completed her master's degree in art history. Ducey is currently pursuing her Ph.D., researching the influence of (Asian) Indian fabrics and culture on early American quilts. In her spare time, she collects quilts and vintage fabrics and continues to learn how to make quilts.

INDEX

Page references in italics indicate illustrations. The fifty-three quilts highlighted from the International Quilt Study Center's collection and their plate numbers are in boldface.